NEW YORK
past and present

Barnes & Noble Books
NEW YORK

NEW YORK
past and present

Texts
Costanza Poli

Art Director
Patrizia Balocco Lovisetti

Graphic Design
Anna Galliani

Translation
Ann Ghiringhelli
C.T.M., Milan

CONTENTS

INTRODUCTION	PAGE 8
FOUR CENTURIES OF HISTORY	PAGE 24
THE CITY WHO TALKS TO THE SKY	PAGE 60
THE BEAT OF "THE BIG APPLE"	PAGE 122
INDEX	PAGE 132

1 The façade of one of the numerous giants of Manhattan looks warped when seen through the futuristic glass wall of a Midtown building.

2/7 This group of allegorical figures (foreground) welcomes passengers at the main entrance to the Grand Central Terminal. In the background we can see a ghost from the past, demolished in 1967 - the Singer Building.

3/6 The Empire State Building is instantly recognized amid the thousands of buildings that crowd Manhattan. It may be nearly seventy years old but - its appeal undiminished - it is still first favourite on tourist itineraries.

© 1998 White Star S.r.l.
Via C. Sassone, 22/24
13100 Vercelli, Italy.

This edition published by
Barnes & Noble, Inc.,
by arrangement with
White Star S.r.l.,
2001 Barnes & Noble Books

All rights reserved. This book, or any portion thereof, may not be reproduced in any form without written permission of the publisher.

ISBN 0-7607-2403-2
M10987654321

Colour separations
by Fotomec, Turin and
Grafiche Mazzucchelli, Milan.
Printed in Italy
by Grafedit, Bergamo.

9 top In this aerial view we can see the very tip of Manhattan Island, hemmed in by the Hudson and East River.

10-11 The towers of the World Trade Center catch the light of the setting sun, creating stunning scenic effects.

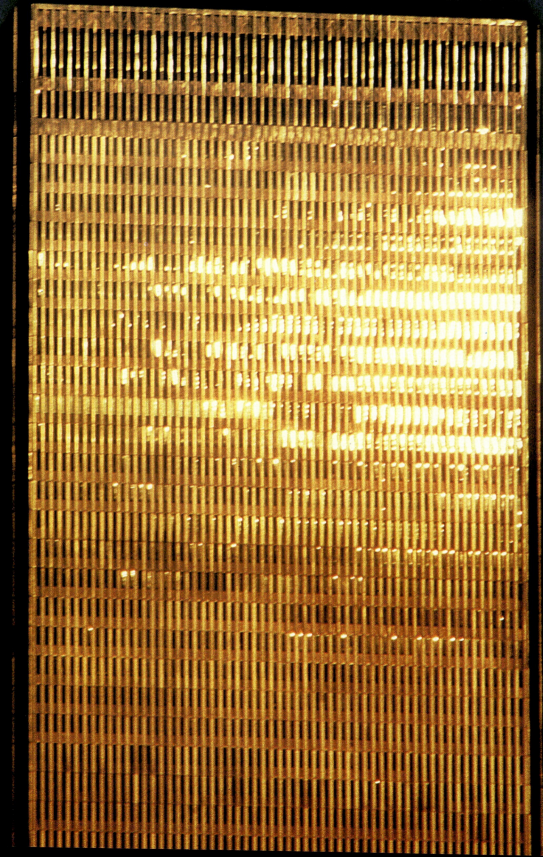

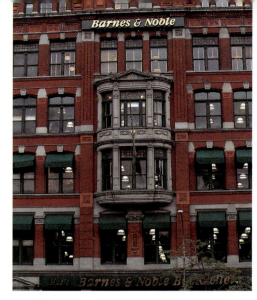

12 top left
The traditional bright yellow of the taxis and the steam puffing out of the manholes are constant features of the chaotic traffic in the American metropolis, "the city that never sleeps" (to quote the very apt lyrics of a famous song about New York).

12 bottom left
The prestigious Waldorf Astoria hotel was built in 1931 on Park Avenue, in Art Deco style. Extensive renovation and refurbishment in the '80s (at a cost of 200 million dollars) left the original ambience intact but brought welcome enhancements to the hotel's facilities.

12 top right *In this façade, we can recognise one of the most famous bookshops of New York - Barnes & Noble.*

Later, a series of circumstances allowed me to renew my acquaintance with New York, for longer and in greater depth. Only then did I begin to realize how much more lay beneath the glossy picture-postcard image. I caught my glimpses of a complex city where life often had to be learnt the hard way, an urban landscape dotted with areas best considered off-limits, a place populated not only by exceptionally friendly New Yorkers but also by people whose behaviour was at best unpredictable: an enlightening insight into real life, for a young European. I sometimes wonder how other first-time visitors reacted to the Big Apple. But I cannot imagine its impact on someone arriving from, say, Costa Rica, Shanghai or Warsaw - not as a tourist but out of need, rather than choice - and confronted with the skyscrapers, the homeless trying to keep warm over the grids of subway air vents, the windows of Tiffany's, the all-night stores where you run into the kind of people that would appeal to Paul Auster. My New York nights were made up of jazz clubs and Thai eateries where it was normal practice to take in a bottle of Californian wine in a paper bag; other people's may have been punctuated by sirens and skirmishes. Everyone probably has their own personal memories, which they cannot and in any case would not change. I firmly believe nonetheless that each individual finds some corner of New York in which to feel at home or, as Woody Allen said in *Manhattan*, something really worth living for, such

12-13 Two mannequins in bathing-suits cast flirtatious glances at the shivering passers-by. This shop window belongs to Macy's, a department store dating back to the start of the 20th century which still retains the fascination of the past, seemingly indifferent to the proliferating shopping malls and retail zones.

13 top A helicopter challenges the imposing solemnity of the twin towers of the World Trade Center, 110 storeys high.

14-15 In Harlem ethnic identity shouts out at every turn, be it in a brightly coloured mural or soul food centred on southern-fried chicken and sweet potatoes.

16 top left The statue of Alma Mater by Daniel Chester French stands in front of the Low Library building at Columbia University. The campus is situated in a lively and culturally vibrant district.

16 top right From ancient times to now, the Metropolitan Museum covers all areas of art and human knowledge. The photograph shows a statue by Canova, of Perseus holding Medusa's head.

16-17 The space in front of the Rockefeller Center, dominated by the giant gilded statue of Prometheus, is used in summer by coffee drinkers, who can imagine themselves in a European square, and by ice skaters in winter.

17 top "They shall beat their swords into plowshares, and their spears into pruning forks: nation shall not lift up sword against nation, neither shall they learn war any more". These words of Isaiah are engraved on the base of a statue by Evgeny Vuchetich, in front of the United Nations Building.

17 bottom The streets of New York often contain unusual modern sculptures. Here we see a work by K. Haring.

as a squirrel running towards you, to gather up nuts you've put down on the grass in Central Park. New York, in fact, offers many sensations to feel. It is pleasing, for instance, to descend the spiral ramp at the Guggenheim, your head a-buzz with Frank Lloyd Wright and Picasso, or to gaze upwards at Mies Van der Rohe's Seagram Building.

Equally surprising is queuing at TKTS, on Broadway, for half-price theatre tickets and suddenly discovering that right beside you is a fellow Italian, who knows at least five ways to get a free meal in New York. More experiences of New York: stamping your feet to fight off the cold while watching the Thanksgiving Day parade, or reading in Columbia University library. Finally, a trip to Coney Island is another way to "feel" the Big Apple and pass the time of day.

18-19 The Statue of Liberty stands on tiny Bedloe's Island, now known as Liberty Island. Towering over the harbour, this most celebrated of New York sights attracts hundreds of thousands of visitors every year. About ten years ago the statue underwent a thorough cleaning operation, at a cost of almost 70 million dollars.

20-21 As evening falls, New York takes on its electrifying nocturnal atmosphere. The skyline is dominated by the towers of the World Trade Center, which cast their reflections in the dark waters of the East River.

FOUR CENTURIES OF HISTORY

The only trace of the Algonquins left in the area we now know as New York is the name of the Algonquin Hotel, home to the city's most eccentric cultural circle of the 1920s. Even before the white men arrived to colonise the southern valley of the Hudson river, the Algonquins had been virtually annihilated by the Iroquois Indians (whose name in the language of their

24 left This print taken from a painting by Charles Bird King shows a Chippeway woman. The bundle she is clutching contains not a child but some of her dead husband's possessions: in keeping with Chippeway custom, widows had to carry the bundle around with them for a whole year, as a sign of mourning.

24 right The two Iroquois Indians in this print taken from a painting by George Catlin are wearing their traditional dress. The area which later became New York was inhabited first by Algonquian Indians and then by the warlike Iroquois who chased them. They lived here in wooden longhouses, growing crops and raising livestock. Their clothes were made from animal hides, often decorated by the womenfolk with elaborate embroidered patterns and glass beads. With the arrival of the Europeans - who brought disease as well as violence and oppression - this world was destroyed for good.

25 top Samuel de Champlain, who led a French expedition to North America in 1603, as well as being the acknowledged founder of French Canada, is remembered for his perseverance in establishing "civilized" relations with the Indians. He wanted not simply to keep the peace: he saw the natives as excellent trading partners; they also knew the territory's physical features and resources and could be used to extend the newcomers' field of action.

25 centre and bottom Relations between settlers and natives were not always peaceful: these old prints show two battle scenes. In the first, Champlain's troops are attacking a camp belonging to Onodaga Indians (one of the six Iroquois nations unified under chief Hiawatha); illustrated in the second is a skirmish in open country between Indian warriors and the French.

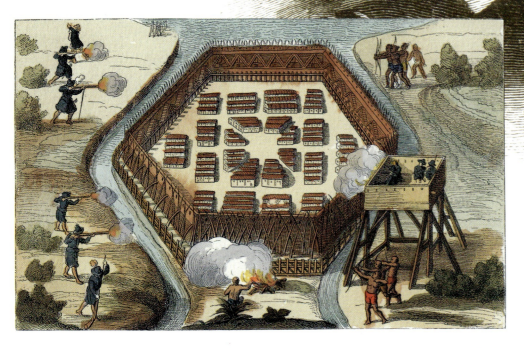

enemies meant "true serpents"). The Iroquois with their highly efficient war machine were, in the words of Charlevoix, a member of the French expedition led by Samuel de Champlain in 1603, "laying the whole of Canada waste". While they easily conquered the Algonquins, their passion for warfare would have led inevitably to their destruction, had at the end of the sixteenth century an enlightened warrior named Hiawatha not recognised the danger facing his people, divided as they were into various tribes. It was then, thanks to the intervention of the Great Spirit who guided him in a dream, inviting him to promote a new unity among the brothers, that Hiawatha created the Iroquois League of Six Nations (Mohawk, Oneida, Onondaga, Cayuga, Seneca and at a later date, Tuscaroras) — a confederation that would perhaps have succeeded in overcoming diversity and living together in peace had they, the white men, not arrived.

26-27 An important moment of Hudson's expedition is here recalled: his meeting with Indians while ascending the navigable stretch of the river that now bears his name. In his ship's logbook Hudson described the natives as polite and friendly; he wrote that they had plentiful provisions, hides and furs and were happy to trade with other peoples.

27 top left This is how the island of Manhattan must have looked before the settlers arrived: thick forests dotted with clearings where the natives had built their longhouses.

27 top right This print shows Hudson being formally assigned his exploratory mission by officials of the Dutch East India Company.

26 top left The English explorer Henry Hudson was in the pay of the Dutch East India Company and he ensured that the Netherlands controlled the future New Amsterdam. The river along the western shores of Manhattan is named after him.

26 top right In 1524 Giovanni da Verrazzano caught sight of the future New York. His visit was brief: a storm almost immediately forced him to head out to sea.

26 bottom left This Chippeway chieftain is wearing the tribe's traditional ceremonial dress. His pipe and feathered head-dress are an indication of high rank.

The first explorer to see the future New York was Giovanni da Verrazzano, an Italian navigator in the service of the French Crown. He set out in 1523 on the orders of Francis I apparently in search of the legendary Northwest Passage towards the Indies. His secret objective was actually to investigate the possibility of a French dominion in the Americas. Giovanni reached the mouth of the strait that is today crossed by a bridge bearing his name but a sudden squall prevented him from exploring the natural harbour. This "brief encounter" was not extended until over eighty years later when the Dutch West India Company sent the *Half Moon* commanded by Henry Hudson to the eastern coasts of the unexplored continent. This was in 1609 and the commander, with less than 20 men, was still searching for the Northwest Passage. They ascended the inlet from the sea and discovered that it was in fact a river that was subsequently to be known as the Hudson. The English navigator's enterprise did not make his fortune: during a successive voyage the crew mutinied and abandoned him alone on a minute boat at the mercy of the freezing Arctic waters. His discovery even failed to arise much interest from his employer and it was not until some years later, in 1613, that the Dutch West India Company decided to exploit its small American possession, in particular for the vast number of valuable fur-bearing animals populating its virgin forests.

The colony, New Amsterdam, really was small and insignificant, composed of two forts, one at New Amsterdam on the island of Manhattan, the other inland at New Albany. Manhattan was officially "acquired" in 1626 for the sum of sixty florins, to which the governor, Peter Minuit, "generously" added a few knick-knacks. The appearance of New Amsterdam was quite different from that of the great city from which it took its name. It was a collection of huts set around a small fort and a windmill and was inhabited by around 300 souls devoted above all to the consumption of alcohol. Animals roamed freely along the muddy streets and there were regular skirmishes with the Indians who continued to live on the island (Broadway, the name of which was derived from that of the Dutchman Breede Wegh, was original-

28 top The scene portrayed in this work by Jonas Bronck is the signing of a treaty between the Dutch and Wickquaesgeek Indians.

28-29 top The Dutch West India Company was established in 1621. One of its first tasks was to build New Amsterdam, on the island of Manhattan. The print shows us how it apparently looked in 1673.

28-29 bottom New Amsterdam was initially no more than a small fort on the very tip of the island, serving essentially as a trading post between the colony and its motherland, the Netherlands.

29 top Depicted here is the seal of New Amsterdam. Although it closely resembles the seal of the Netherlands' old capital, completing the new emblem is a beaver, a creature then typically found in the waters of the Hudson, flowing into the sea at New Amsterdam.

ly an Algonquin track known as Weekquaesgeek).

Things changed in 1647 with the arrival of a new governor, Peter Stuyvesant. An austere, strict man, Stuyvesant was ill-inclined to tolerate the life style of his compatriots who built their houses with no thought as to planning (Lower Manhattan is still distinguished from the rest of the island by its tortuous streets). To no great avail he attempted to impose severe rules such as a nine o'clock closure for the taverns — of which at that time there were said to be one for every twelve men — and ordered a defensive wall to be constructed: the road that ran along the wall eventually became Wall Street, the present-day symbol of the world of high finance. Amidst such disorder, one factor that had the potential to attract new colonists was religious tolerance. The New Netherlands made no distinction between the Catholics, Protestants, Quakers and Jews who began to arrive from 1654. Stuyvesant tried to oppose the wave of immigration in the name of national unity but fortunately his proposal to deport all the new arrivals was ignored. He consoled himself by paving the streets of the colony, constructing the first hospital and passing decrees whereby under his supervision the rustic appearance of the buildings was improved and they began to resemble those of the mother country. Nevertheless, all his efforts eventually proved to be in vain. The fur trade was not sufficiently profitable according to the calculations of the Dutch West India Company and nobody in Holland appeared willing to fight to maintain the outpost.

29 centre This plan of the city was produced in 1660 by Jacques Cortelyou, then governor-general of New Amsterdam.

29 bottom Peter Stuyvesant arrived in the colonies in 1647. He introduced strict laws and promoted many initiatives designed to improve the life of settlers.

30 left Charles II of England gained control of New Amsterdam in 1664, when troops under colonel Richard Nicolls took over the city. The king gave the colony to his brother James, Duke of York, who promptly changed its name. New York, future "queen" of the 20th century, thus came into being.

30 right Jacob Leisler, a rich merchant, made his mark on New York's history towards the end of the 17th century when, supported by other settlers, especially those of Dutch origin, he took charge of the colony and assumed the title of lieutenant governor. During his almost two years of government he set out to obtain independence from England (which had taken control of New Amsterdam some years before), for mainly economic reasons. But the British crown eventually sent troops and Leisler, together with nine of his supporters, was convicted and hanged. At this time 93 cannons were installed to protect the precious colony, in the area still known today as the Battery.

30-31 By the 18th century New York was already well on the way to becoming a metropolis. Admittedly only a very small part of Manhattan Island was inhabited and fortified, but the harbour was constantly buzzing with activity as big ships sailed to and fro, to Europe and the West Indies, carrying with them different cultures and languages as well as men and merchandise.

It was thus that in 1664 four British ships commanded by Richard Nicolls succeeded in conquering New Amsterdam without a shot being fired. Only Peter Stuyvesant attempted to stand up to the invaders, vocally demonstrating his opposition. The King of England at the time, Charles II, gifted the new colony to his brother, the Duke of York. This was the end of New Amsterdam and the birth of New York. The city was still restricted in size, clinging to the southern tip of the island of Manhattan. Many of the 10,000 or so inhabitants still worked the land, while a small proportion of them was involved in the fur trade. As in Britain, the agricultural system was based on large estates and in contrast with the centuries-later situation, the main problem facing the great landowners was finding workers willing to leave the fields of Europe to cultivate those of the New World. The centralising policy of the new conquerors aroused the opposition of the immigrants who rebelled in 1689 and, led by Jacob Lester, took control of the city. Lester, appointing himself as chairman of the Committee of Public Health, succeeded in running the city for almost two years, backed by the old Dutch bourgeoisie but opposed by the representatives of the British Crown. The rebellion was eventually crushed and independence from England was not spoken of again until the American Revolution. Shortly after the end of the revolt, in 1693, 92 cannons were installed to defend the city in the area still known as the Battery; New York had begun to be seen as a place worth defending. In spite of its rather discouraging beginning, the English rule had positive effects on the development of the colony and in the eighteenth century its population increased, leading to the construction of new dwellings and a shift in the location of industrial premises. At that time New York was the capital of the grain milling industry, but ship building also played a prominent role.

In 1702 a new governor arrived from the mother country, Lord Cornbury, a cousin of Queen Anne and so fond of her as to wear, even in public, the most

31 left Only Peter Stuyvesant, stern Dutch governor of New Amsterdam, tried to resist seizure of the city by the English. With a clamorous but pointless gesture, he tore to pieces the letter in which Nicolls appealed to the citizens to surrender without fighting. In this print we see Stuyvesant after the surrender, leaving the city at the head of its troops.

VUE DE LA NOUVELLE YORCK.

32 top In 1748 Frederick Van Cortlandt, a wealthy New Yorker, had a home built in a then rural area (the present-day Bronx). Constructed in typical Georgian-colonial style, Van Cortlandt House is now a museum with a fine collection of period furnishings and household goods, as well as earthenware pottery from Delft.

32-33 Depicted here is a scene from the trial of Peter Zenger, publisher and editor of the New York Weekly Journal, *who was charged with libel after making very strong attacks on the government led by Cosby. The case became famous: Zenger's acquittal endorsed the freedom of the press and introduced the then revolutionary idea that individuals involved in government should be accountable to the entire community for their actions.*

33 top Columbia University is one of the oldest centres of learning in the U.S.A. Founded in 1754, it was initially called King's College.

33 bottom Illustrated in this old print is one of the first classes held at King's College, by William Johnson.

sophisticated outfits of his august relation. Cornbury was despised and disliked by the population, but never as much as one of his successors, Cosby, the target of harsh criticism from the *New York Weekly Journal* founded in 1732 by John Peter Zenger. The periodical has an important place in the history of the city in that it was the first of a plethora of newspapers that recounted over the following centuries local, national and international events, but above all because its founder was to become the champion of the freedom of the press. In that era, in fact, the sole authorised source of information was the *New York Gazette*, a "puff" published by the British government. Zenger rebelled against this monopoly and boldly attacked the governor, frequently allowing him to be portrayed in scathing cartoons. In 1734 the exasperated Cosby had the journalist arrested and accused of libel. Zender was however acquitted in a historic verdict that finally brought the freedom of the press to the colony. In the meantime New York strained to reach European standards of civilisation (with the inauguration of the first theatre and the construction of sophisticated mansions such as Van Cortland House, currently a museum but then a suburban villa in what is now the Bronx) whilst showing signs of the problems faced by all large cities. Prostitutes had elected the Battery as their terrain of choice, epidemics such as the outbreak of smallpox in 1731 mowed down victims due to the disastrous hygiene conditions and the scarcity of water, and in 1741 a wild rumour that the black slaves were rebelling and killing their white masters provoked widespread panic. Thirty-one slaves were killed and around 150 were thrown into prison. One of America's oldest universities, Columbia, then known as King's College, was founded in the middle of the century, but the period also saw the outbreak of the war against the Franco-Indian alliance. The conflict was to a large extent the result of the fur traders' need to find new forests in which to hunt. The British forces eventually succeeded in overcoming their enemies thanks in part to the support of the Iroquois who joined them as a result of the work of William Johnson, the Commissioner for Indian Affairs. His was a significant contribution to the signing of the Treaty of Paris of 1763 that definitively excluded the French from the colonies.

34 top Introduction of the British Stamp Act, a law imposing payment of duty on legal documents, newspapers and playing cards, met with protests from the people of New York State.

34 centre The introduction of the Stamp Act caused riots and uprisings. James McEvers, stamp-duty distributor, resigned from his office, scared by the vehemence of New Yorkers; the revolutionaries took the name "Children of Freedom".

34 bottom Revolutionaries organized rallies near City Park Hall, beside a tree later known as the Liberty Tree. The rallies were attended by numerous patriots ready to revolt against the English crown.

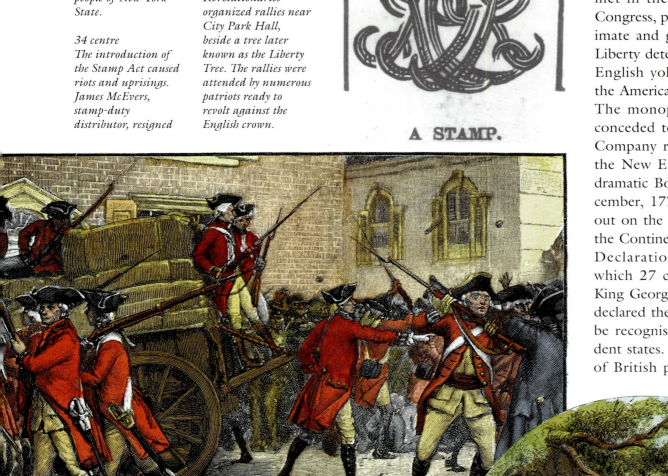

that broke the camel's back was the Stamp Act, a law that imposed taxes on documents, newspapers and playing cards. The New Yorkers were not slow to demonstrate their opposition: delegates from 13 colonies met in the city as the Stamp Act Congress, proclaimed the law illegitimate and gave rise to the Sons of Liberty determined to throw off the English yoke. This was the eve of the American War of Independence. The monopoly on the sale of tea conceded to the British East India Company resulted in the revolt of the New England traders with the dramatic Boston Tea Party (16 December, 1773). True warfare broke out on the 4th of July, 1776, when the Continental Congress issued the Declaration of Independence in which 27 charges were levelled at King George II and which solemnly declared the right of the colonies to be recognised as free and independent states. New York, as the centre of British power, immediately be-

New York benefited greatly from the war thanks to its strategic position as a bridgehead between Europe and the New World and a gateway to the interior, and as a centre of legalised piracy. The British Crown now had further motives for defending its property but the embrace of the mother country began to be irksome to many New Yorkers who began to harbour thoughts of independence. Britain's reaction could hardly have been less sensitive as it began to tax the colonies, imposing controlled importation and levies for the maintenance of the troops. However, the straw

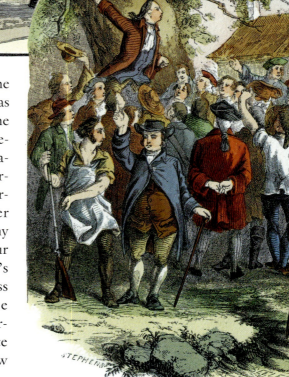

35 top left The Declaration of Independence was made in Philadelphia in 1776, while America's war against the British was still in progress.

35 top right George Washington, general of the American revolutionaries and future president, led fierce battles in and around New York.

35 bottom "My only regret is that I have but one life to lose for my country": these are reportedly the last words spoken by Nathan Hale, a patriot hanged by the British.

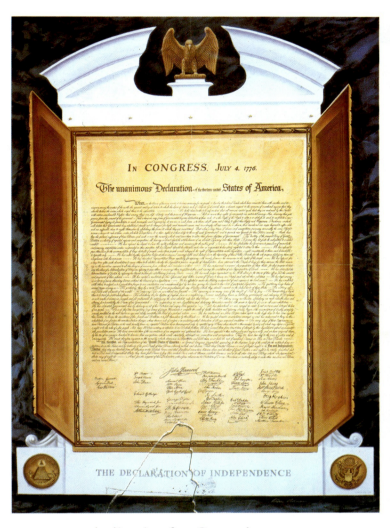

came a symbolic city for General George Washington but failing to conquer it, he preferred to leave it for the time being in the hands of the enemy. Up until 1783, the year in which the Treaty of Paris proclaimed the independence of the American colonies, British troops continued to be stationed at New York; only once they had been withdrawn did Washington return to the city that had seen him defeated (at the Battle of Richmond). It had been a difficult period that had seen an enormous increase in the cost of living, fires and summary trials, but also moments of stirring heroism like that demonstrated by the young Nathan Hale and the patriots destined for deportation who perished in the sinking of prison ships.

36 top The statue of King George III was too strong a symbol of British power to be left standing on its pedestal.

36 bottom Fires had always been a very real threat to New York. In September 1776 the fire started by the rebels before retreating from the city destroyed Trinity Church and burnt about 1,000 houses to the ground.

37 left Visible in this old map are sites where the battle of Long Island was fought in 1776.

37 top right At the battle of Long Island British general William Howe forced Washington to retreat. But the American patriots did not lose heart and before long scored a major victory at Harlem Heights.

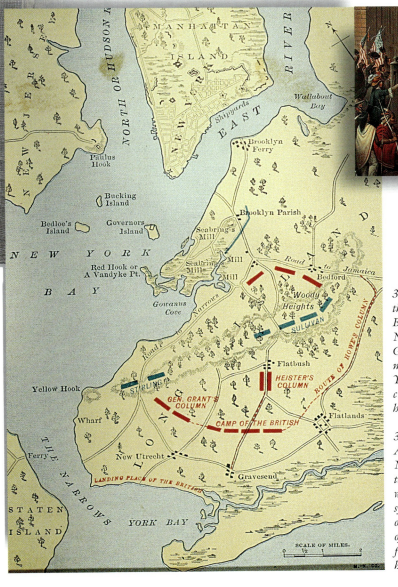

37 centre right After the withdrawal of British troops, on November 25, 1783 George Washington marched into New York. The people of the city afforded him a hero's welcome.

37 bottom right As British troops leave New York harbour, the Stars and Stripes - with 13 stars symbolizing the original member states of the Federation - flutters from the highest flagpole.

38 top History is also made by single symbolic episodes: in this print we see Governor De Witt Clinton of New York pouring a bottle of water from Lake Erie into the Atlantic Ocean, to mark the opening of the canal linking the two. The inauguration of the Erie Canal in 1815 turned New York's harbour into a major seaport for the country's vast inland regions.

38-39 The picture shows Lockport in the Erie Canal which was constructed on the initiative of Gov. De Witt Clinton. New York's rivers and waterways have played a determining part in the city's commercial success.

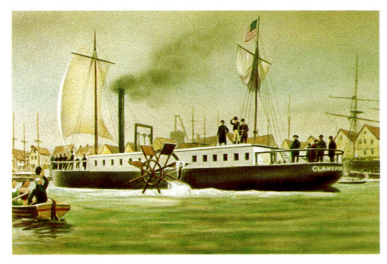

39 top 1807 saw the launch of the Clermont, *the first of the steamboats invented by Robert Fulton. Fast and easy to manoeuvre, these steamboats helped make the port of New York even more important for trade with America's inland regions, the West, and with Europe.*

39 centre Bryant Park, at the rear of New York Public Library, was once known as Reservoir Park. In 1853 the first international exposition was held in the Crystal Palace, sadly destroyed by fire only five years later.

39 bottom An old print shows Broadway in the mid-19th century. This glittering hub of the New York entertainment scene, now lined with theatres and clubs, was once an Indian trail. It was widened by Dutch colonists who called it by the Dutch name Breetweg.

New York in the late eighteenth century had over 33,000 inhabitants. For a brief period it had been the capital of the United States but the heavy demands of the War of Independence left it on its knees. It was however ready to bounce back and introduce the changes that were to result in it becoming the cosmopolitan city we know today. The rapid urban expansion was not regulated until 1881 when the Common Council adopted the characteristic grid pattern, but New York markets boomed and the bases were laid for great fortunes. The governor De Witt Clinton associated his name with that of the Erie Canal linking the Great Lakes with Albany, the capital of the state of New York, thus opening up an important communication route between the Midwest and the Atlantic port.

At the same time New York overtook Boston and Philadelphia in terms of importance, becoming the capital of the grain and foodstuffs markets. With its natural advantages, New York's port was to remain the world's greatest until the 1960's when Rotterdam assumed the mantle. The shipyards prospered and in 1807 Robert Fulton launched his first steamship, the *Clermont*, a type of vessel particularly well suited to river traffic. With its old defensive role now obsolete, Wall Street became the nerve-centre of American capitalism. In the meantime the city adopted the trappings of modernity. In 1832 a public transport system was introduced using horse-drawn omnibuses that remained in service for almost a century; brownstones, the single-family homes in brown sandstone that are so typical of the city began to be constructed; the Crystal Palace exhibition hall was built in 1853 and like its "twin" in London was destroyed in a fire some years later. Macy's, the prototype American department store selling anything to anybody was founded in 1858.

39

40 top left Andrew Carnegie emigrated to the USA from Scotland as a very young man and eventually became a steel magnate. The enormous riches he accumulated - mainly from railroad construction - made it possible for him to become one of the greatest philanthropists and benefactors of his era.

40 top right On September 15, 1890 work started on building Carnegie Hall, the concert hall that was home to the New York Philarmonic Orchestra. As this picture shows, the foundation stone was laid in the presence of Andrew Carnegie. Ten years later he retired from business, leaving his empire in the hands of Pierpont Morgan.

41 top According to people in the know, Carnegie Hall's acoustics are outstanding. There's no denying that the very greatest orchestras conducted by legendary figures of 20th-century music, from Toscanini to Bernstein, have played in this huge, austere-looking edifice: Tchaikovsky, no less, was conductor at the inauguration concert in 1891. Today big names from the world of modern music as well as classical performers appear at Carnegie Hall (housed under the same roof is the Weill Recital Hall, plus a museum with exhibits attesting to illustrious guest performers of the past). A national landmark since 1964, the hall underwent extensive renovation in 1986.

In the second half of the century the city's great and wealthy found spectacular means of exhibiting their power. This was New York's golden age, with great magnates such as Andrew Carnegie who donated a grandiose auditorium, Carnegie Hall, to the city, or who began to construct the modern pyramids, the skyscrapers. Chicago had already seen the raising of vast edifices but it was in New York that they reached their apotheosis. The wives of the magnates spent the riches of their consorts on Fashion Row, the stretch of Sixth Avenue on which the most elegant boutiques are concentrated, and wore the clothes they purchased to the exclusive parties described in the stories and novels of Edith Wharton that bring to life a Puritan world in which the demon of "vulgarity" was beginning to make its presence felt. The other side of the coin, however, revealed a far less attractive New York. While the city was the "moral", or rather "economic" capital of the United States and provided avant-garde services (the construction of the elevated railway began in the 1870s, in 1877 the inventor Alexander Graham Bell demonstrated for the first time the potential of a new invention, the telephone, and in 1880 the city's first electric street lighting was inaugurated), it was also the scene of great contrasts.

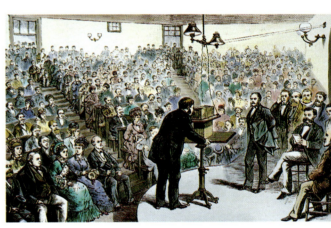

40-41 This view of New York dates back to around 1850: on the right are Brooklyn and the piers of Manhattan Island. The city's providential position - at the mouth of two navigable rivers flowing into the Atlantic Ocean - allowed its harbour to play a key role in trade between America and Europe.

41 right Scottish-born Alexander Graham Bell was an "accidental inventor". In 1876, during experiments aimed essentially at teaching speech to the deaf-and-dumb, conducted while he was professor of vocal physiology at Boston University, he created a device that subsequently changed the history of communications: the telephone. Two other inventors, Meucci and Gray, arrived at his same conclusions around the same time. One of the first demonstrations of Bell's invention can be seen in the print above.

42 top left By the end of the 19th century New York could be classified as a metropolis. Part of the fortunes made by entrepreneurs and merchants was invested in further property development and the city continued to grow, with the green expanse of Central Park at its centre. During these years important additions were made to the urban landscape: in 1892, for instance (the year of this city map), construction work began on the cathedral of St. John the Divine and Ellis Island opened its doors to the first of many thousands of immigrants.

42 centre left Elevated railroads, above the city streets, became a necessity in the second half of the 1800s.

42 bottom A station was built on the site in 1871 by Cornelius Vanderbilt but the Grand Central Terminal we see today, in splendid Beaux Arts style, dates to 1913.

42-43 This Currier & Ives view of New York harbour, dated 1878, presents an animated scene: bustling crowds, numerous sailing ships and steamboats, carts and carriages hurrying to and fro. The city was meanwhile spreading further and further inland, to accommodate new inhabitants arriving from Europe.

43 bottom left Brooklyn Bridge was opened in 1883, in the presence of the authorities and huge, wildly enthusiastic crowds.

right This old illustration gives a clear idea of the courage and daring of the workmen who helped build Brooklyn Bridge in the second half of the 19th century. Operating conditions were hazardous and only the very bravest workers could handle the job of fixing the very high vertical suspender cables. Designed by John Roebling and completed in 1883, the bridge claimed about 20 lives, lost through falls or the bends after underwater excavation work on the foundations. Now, over a century later, the "steel harp" continues to be an emblem of New York, as well as one of the main links between Manhattan and Brooklyn. A walk along the elevated promenade offers stunning views and pedestrians feel very small and insignificant beside this giant masterpiece of engineering.

44 top One of New York's best known symbols, the Statue of Liberty, was a gift to the people of America from the French. Its unveiling by President Grover Cleveland on October 28, 1886 was celebrated with great enthusiasm.

44 centre This photo shows New York harbour at the end of the last century. After an extensive restructuring scheme, the hustle and bustle typical of this part of New York in the gilded years has now returned. A museum housed in old warehouse buildings offers an overview of the city's maritime history.

44 bottom Bethesda Fountain, in Central Park, is named after a figure from the Bible. Inaugurated in 1873, it very quickly became one of the spots New Yorkers like to make for when strolling in the vast green spaces of the park.

45 top left Broadway is the only street "out of sync" within New York's perfect urban grid. About 25 kilometres long, it continues beyond the city boundary as far as Albany, state capital, testifying to an old Indian trail.

45 top right Macy's is much more than a department store: others may offer more prestigious goods, but none can beat it for popularity. It started life as a small shop but is now so huge it covers an entire block. This photograph shows the horse-drawn carts used by Macy's for home deliveries in the 19th century.

45 bottom Depicted here is the elevated railroad at Coenties Slip. When, in 1868, Charles T. Harvey offered the first demonstration of an elevated train running on rails, many New Yorkers were willing to bet the carriages would go crashing into the street below. The system instead proved a success and in 1902 the lines were electrified. Nowadays most commuters use the city's very extensive subway system, with lines reaching the Bronx, Queens and Brooklyn.

46 left After a long and exhausting voyage, made in conditions of extreme discomfort and hardship (top and centre picture), immigrants disembarked on Ellis Island (bottom picture) where they underwent a thorough medical examination, to avoid the risk of epidemics.

New York attracted masses of European emigrants with a mirage of easy pickings; to those who arrived from the hovels of the Old Continent, however, the new Mecca really had very little to offer: low wages, squalid and frighteningly overcrowded living conditions. In 1892 the authorities opened Ellis Island, the "Gateway to America" that was not to close until 1954. Here the new arrivals were examined by doctors who had the power to repatriate them if they found symptoms of infectious diseases; their impoverished be-

longings were searched; families ran the risk of being divided. The Island of Tears, now the home to the Museum of Immigration, was for many their first contact with a situation that was far harsher than they could have imagined. Fear of the New World encouraged many to seek refuge in close-knit national communities, thus giving rise to the various quarters that still maintain a strong ethnic identity; take, for example, Little Italy with its pizzerias and feast day in honour of San Gennaro, or the Lower East Side, a home far from home

46 top right Christmas spent on Ellis Island could be a celebration at the start of a new life or, after refusal of entry, a dismal period spent waiting to make the journey back home. Ellis Island was in operation for 62 years and about 17 million people passed through its gates.

46 bottom right This picture shows a tenement house around the year 1870. Many immigrants had no option but to live in these overcrowded slums, often lacking windows and air shafts. Most of these tenements were located in Lower East Side where, at the turn of the century, population density was five times higher than in other districts of New York.

for thousands of Jews who had fled from eastern Europe. According to a census made in 1890 the latter quarter proved to be the most densely populated area in the world with almost a thousand people crowded into each acre, thus beating even Bombay. The dwellings, lacking private sanitary facilities, housed a community perpetually struggling for their daily bread. The European ghettos had to all intents and purposes been reconstructed, with the difference that those in New York housed not only people of the Jewish faith, but a

47 left As is clearly evident from this photo - taken in 1924 in the Bronx, at the corner of Clay and Findely Avenue - crossing an ocean did little to change many aspects of immigrants' lifestyles. Between the high buildings where families and families crowded, washing stretched across the street looked like flags on a dressed ship in harbour.

large proportion of the total number of emigrants. This overcrowding led to a change in the urban structure of the city; the reasonably well-off families still chose row houses, the "English-style" terraced brownstones. Soon however, the houses began to be divided into apartments while the poorest section of the population, the workers and the immigrants, were packed into tenements. These vast warrens had shared lavatories, no central heating and in some cases even lacked windows.

A normal member of the middle-classes would never have agreed to live in such overcrowded, unhygienic conditions. However, the lack of building land obliged even the wealthy to accept hitherto unthinkable solutions, and in the most exclusive quarters, with views over Central Park, huge, luxurious buildings were constructed that still today are at the top of the wish lists of many New Yorkers.

A classic example is the Dakota building on 72nd Street, famous in this century as the home of John Lennon; he was murdered just in front of the entrance.

47 right The various ethnic groups that populated different quarters of New York are easily recognized in these pictures: from the Jewish immigrants in Hester Street (top) to the Italians in Mulberry Street (centre and bottom).

In the meantime public life was forced to acknowledge the new socio-ethnic make-up of the city, but the results were hardly encouraging. The name of William "Boss" Tweed, a devious lobbyist who managed to gain control of the city, is still associated with political manipulation and corruption. From Tammany Hall, Tweed succeeded in raking in millions of dollars, diverting municipal funds and profiting for contracts awarded for the great public works. A typical example was the construction of the so-called Tweed Courthouse that cost 14 million dollars, 9 million of them ending up in the politician's pocket. The new century was to cement New York's reputation as the metropolis par excellence. In 1898 the five districts, Manhattan, Queens, Brooklyn, Richmond and the Bronx, were united, the resulting city having around 3 million inhabitants and was home to around 70% of the most influential companies in the country.

Its port was capable of handling three quarters of the goods imported into the United States and almost half of those exported. Capital flowed into the city and the skyscrapers thrust ever higher as the immigrants continued to throng through the gates of paradise.

48 top The story of William March Tweed, known by one and all as "Boss" Tweed, shows that corruption does not pay: although he escaped from prison and fled to Spain, he was eventually recaptured and died back in gaol.

48 centre The County Court House was intended to be "Boss" Tweed's biggest and best swindle: no less than 9 million dollars of the 14 million demanded for its construction ended up in the pockets of wheeler-dealing Tweed.

48 bottom A fire at the Triangle Shirtwaist Company in 1911 claimed the lives of 146 workers. The tragedy triggered a series of reforms to improve working conditions.

48-49 This picture, taken by the American photographer Lewis W. Hine around 1920, shows a group of newsboys. In those years it was by no means unusual to see young children working.

49 bottom This old photo was taken inside a vegetable-canning factory. In a place like this women and children made ideal workers; their wages were also much lower than men's.

In the factories, the women and children worked from dawn to dusk, earning barely enough on which to survive, before returning to residential quarters oppressed by suffocating heat or bitter cold. In 1911 a fire at the Triangle Shirtwaist Company killed 146 workers; it was only in the wake of this tragedy that the authorities finally decided that reform was urgently required to ensure a degree of safety for workers, to defend the weak and to provide a statutory day of rest for all. The enormous statue that in 1886 had been presented to the American people by France, the Statue of Liberty, finally began to make some sense.

50 top left New York traffic was already chaotic in the early 1900s. This photo shows a typical street scene: cars, streetcars and pedestrians crowding the sidewalk in front of a post office.

50 bottom left The Flatiron Building, originally known as the Fuller Building, was completed in 1902 to a project by D.H. Burnham. It's said that city idlers got into the habit of hanging around outside it, in the hope that a gust of wind - created by the building's shape - might blow up the skirts of passing girls and reveal their ankles.

50 centre The Singer Building, built by Ernest Flagg in 1908 at Broadway and John Street, held the title of tallest skyscraper in town for only 18 months. It was demolished in 1967.

50 top right The Ausonia Hotel was built in 1900 at 56th Street and 7th Avenue, to a project by H.J. Hardenbergh. Its design was clearly influenced by the Beaux Arts style, in America often interpreted with opulent use of ornamentation.

50 bottom right In this early 1900s photo we see the Fifth Avenue colonnade and the arch erected as a tribute to George Dewey, hero of the Spanish-American War.

51 top The U.S. Custom House was completed in 1907 at a cost of over 7 million dollars. The four statues along its façade represent the continents of Asia, America, Europe and Africa.

51 centre At the beginning of the century Wall Street was already the financial heart of the city. New York was in fact founded right here and George Washington was sworn as first president of the United States next to the present Federal Hall, now a national monument.

51 bottom left With the millions of five-cent coins people spent in his stores, Frank Woolworth made a fortune. The headquarters of his empire were located in the Gothic-style skyscraper that bears his name, overlooking City Hall Park.

51 bottom right This huge metal skeleton can already be identified as the Woolworth Building, completed in 1913.

After the Great War it was Prohibition that began to influence the direction taken by city life. The first result of the 18th Amendment that banned alcohol was a proliferation of clandestine stills and smuggling. The gangsters established their power bases and the police force was split into two camps: honest cops and those willing to collaborate with the underworld. James J. Walker, a man more interested in his private affairs than those of the city, was elected mayor in 1926. When, in 1930, the Seabury Commission began a massive investigation into civic corruption one of its principal targets was

52 top left Prohibition lasted fourteen years, from 1919 to 1933. The Eighteenth Amendment of the Constitution banned production, sale, transport and importation of alcoholic beverages, and the Volstead Act made their possession a punishable offence too. Thousands of New York bars were closed but their place was taken by countless speakeasies (illegal liquor outlets).

52 bottom left This type of waistcoat was very fashinable with bootleggers during the Prohibition years.

52 top right All kinds of subterfuge were used to serve alcoholic drink: this photo shows the cellars of the Pennsylvania Hotel, where soft drink bottles were emptied and filled with liquor.

*52 bottom right
Like the famous gangster Al Capone, Arthur Flegenheimer - king of brewers - was accused of tax evasion and imprisoned; he was later released on payment of bail (75,000 dollars!).*

53 left The end of Prohibition was naturally celebrated with plenty of hard drinking. For bootleggers, however, the days of big money and easy earnings were over.

*53 top right
The flamboyant Jimmy "Beau James" Walker was elected mayor in 1926. He resigned from office in 1932 after serious corruption scandals, leaving the city with debts of almost 2 billion dollars.*

*53 bottom right
The Wall Street crash of 1929 brought the country to the verge of collapse. It was Franklin Delano Roosevelt, with the New Deal, who eventually steered U.S. towards a new era of prosperity. This picture gives an idea of the drama of those days, when people reduced to poverty filled the city streets.*

the mayor himself. In a celebrated episode $360,000 were found in a jar in his kitchen. His life savings? When Walker resigned in 1932 New York was reeling under the weight of unimaginable debt. In the meantime the Wall Street stock market, the financial heart of the nation, had collapsed leaving millions of newly impoverished people in its wake. The unemployment, poverty and hunger that appeared to have been defeated during the Roaring Twenties when the music of Cab Calloway poured out of the Cotton Club and Babe Ruth sent crowds wild with his feats on the baseball field, were the trademarks of the Depression.

54 top left Franklin Delano Roosevelt, governor of New York State, shakes the hand of Al Smith, his predecessor, during the Democratic Convention in Albany.

54 top right The hardship caused by the Depression was at its most severe around 1936 when this demonstration by jobless workers took place: at that time about half the male population was unemployed.

The governor of the state of New York, Franklin Delano Roosevelt, who was subsequently to become president of the United States, showed his mettle in founding what may be seen as the prototype of the New Deal, the Temporary Emergency Relief Administration, thanks to which the most pressing problems could be tackled.

Once elected president, Roosevelt continued his efforts in favour of his city by permitting a series of public works projects to get underway that helped to alleviate unemployment.

In 1933 a man destined to make a profound impression on the city was elected mayor, Fiorello La Guardia. Born to a Jewish mother and an Italian father, blessed with great personality and innate cordiality, Little Flower was probably the New Yorkers' best loved First Citizen. Not only did he commit himself to eradicating violence and corruption within the public administration, but it was thanks to him that the city began to take on the appearance we know today. Whilst La Guardia inaugurated parks, and great buildings destined to take a place in history, such as the Rockefeller Center and the Empire State Building, were being constructed, in Europe Fascism and Nazism were challenging the world-wide balance of power. In 1941 the United States officially went to war.

54-55 This was how the skyscrapers of New York looked to the members of the Zeppelin airship in 1924.

55 top Fiorello La Guardia, "Little Flower", was a tremendously popular mayor of New York. Son of an Italian father and a Jewish mother, he was an amalgam of the very finest qualities produced by the melting pot; he spoke a number of languages and was loved by one and all. In the space of six years he put the house of New York in order and gave a new boost to construction in both public and private sectors.

55 bottom In 1929 the Chrysler Building added a soaring new landmark to New York's celebrated skyline.

56 left The scene in this photo was immortalized during the construction of the Empire State Building. There's no denying that safety systems for workers still left much room for improvement!

56-57 This group of workmen found an unusual spot for their lunch break: the metal girders of the RCA Building, then under construction.

56 bottom A construction worker employed on the Empire State Building offers us a breathtaking demonstration of his sense of balance. Towering skywards, this 102-storey giant has provided the backdrop for numerous films, from King Kong *to* Sleepless in Seattle.

57 top left The small white dot just visible above the RCA Building is one of the first helicopters to have flown in the skies of New York. The occasion was the completion of the building's framework.

57 bottom left The very last bolt on a building in the Rockefeller Center is fixed in place by John D. Rockefeller, Jr. himself.

57 top right This photo takes us back to the ceremony held to mark the opening of the Empire State Building. The project by Shreve, Lamb and Harmon was awarded the 1931 Architectural League Gold Medal, mainly on account of its innovative design features.

57 bottom right Lee Lawrie's statue of Atlas has pride of place in front of the International Building of the Rockefeller Center.

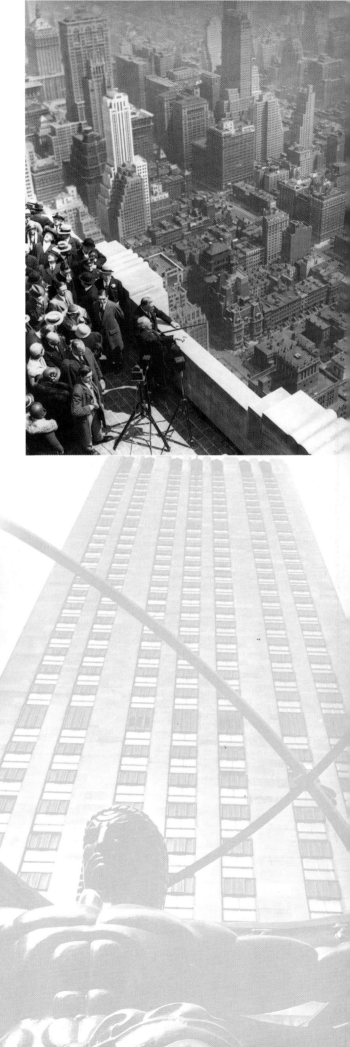

58 top In this picture we see the seemingly never-ending piers along the port of Brooklyn, and the island of Manhattan between the Hudson and East River. The photo, taken in 1971, tells us more than any wordy description could.

*58 bottom
The imposing Queensboro Bridge, straddling Sutton Place, carries traffic over Roosevelt Island and on into Queens. Its construction cost almost 21 million dollars.*

59 top left Ed Koch was mayor of New York from 1980 to 1989. He faced many problems during his period of office, not least - in 1986 - an accusation of corruption in his administration.

59 centre left Mario Cuomo, governor of Italian origins of New York State, has led a determined battle against crime and corruption; he has often been suggested as a possible candidate for the office of president of the United States.

59 bottom left In 1987 another crisis hits Wall Street and stock market prices tumble: panic reigns as operators recall the economic boom of the early Eighties when it seemed nothing could contain soaring stock prices and the city's yuppies, so effectively portrayed by Tom Wolfe in Bonfire of the Vanities.

59 top right David Dinkins, with the support of the Democrats, was the first black mayor to be elected in New York.

Following the Second World War, New York was subjected to radical change, above all due to the third great wave of immigrants, this time arriving above all from the centre and south of the American continent. The metropolis that La Guardia wanted to green, was in fact a slave to the asphalt grid that began to show it defects. The luxury of central Manhattan was countered by the degradation and violence of Harlem, the high-fliers of Wall Street by the new Americans struggling for their very survival. There were moments of splendour and periods of high drama, as in 1975 when a federal loan was necessary to save the administration of the world's richest city from bankruptcy. The renaissance of New York can be dated from the early Eighties with the election of Ed Koch as mayor and Mario Cuomo as state governor. The Big Apple, in spite of the strikes, the urban decay, the arguments, the scandal that in 1986 swept through Koch's administration and the Wall Street collapse of 1987, became the acknowledged capital of the yuppies, the successful young lions described with telling mastery by Tom Wolfe in *The Bonfire of the Vanities*. The great concerts in Central Park, its fame as a melting pot of races and cultures, the spirit of the great artists who elected it as the centre of the creative universe, all attracted millions of visitors and tourists. In 1989 David Dinkins was elected as the city's first black mayor, whilst in 1993 the position was held by Rudolph Giuliani of Italian origins, a former magistrate involved in the struggle against the Mafia and criminality. Someone once said that New York is an "immensely large village": it is time we began to explore it.

59 bottom right After 24 years of Democratic government, in 1993 Rudolph Giuliani won the post of first citizen for the Republicans. Since re-elected (1997), he has succeeded in the challenging task of reducing New York crime rates.

THE CITY THAT TALKS TO THE SKY

60 top left The island of Manhattan, 22 kilometres long and 4 wide, is situated at the point where the Hudson, East River and New York Bay meet.

60 bottom left and 61 The Statue of Liberty which was given by French people to the Americans, to celebrate the alliance between the two peoples during the America's War of Independence, stands on tiny Bedloe's Island. This patch of land was called Minissais (meaning "minor island") by the native Indians, then re-named Great Oyster Island by the early settlers. It acquired its present name from its first white owner, Isaac Bedloe; his widow sold it in 1676 for "81 pounds of Boston money".

S een from above, Manhattan Island looks like a ship determined to break loose from nature's hold and head for the open sea and the world beyond. Instead, the great wide world has come to her, in the form of millions of immigrants who through the years have totally changed her physiognomy, bringing new languages, new colours, new tastes and even a new shape. The bow of this imaginary vessel is Lower Manhattan but first, signalling the presence of the great ship herself, come a tender and a figure-head: Ellis Island and the Statue of Liberty. Between 1892 and 1954 some 17 million people passed through Ellis Island. For many it became, with good reason, the Island of Tears: the Italians, Irish, Poles and Russians who disembarked with their meagre possessions were "processed" and - if medical examination revealed suspicion of contagious disease - turned away. From here however many made their way to the vast interior or took the great leap towards California. But large numbers headed for Little Italy or Brooklyn, perhaps awaited by relations and friends who had come on earlier ships and were now fully-fledged "Americans". In 1990 the long-abandoned island was reopened to the public. After major restructuring at a cost of 156 million dollars, it is now a huge museum in which the story of millions of lives is told. From Ellis Island you can see the Statue of Liberty. Nowadays the great figure is generally regarded as a kind of non-sectarian immigrants' Madonna (a perception endorsed by lines from Emma Lazarus's famous poem, engraved on the base at the beginning of the century: "Give me your tired, your poor, your huddled masses yearning to breathe free"). In actual fact, Frédéric-Auguste Bartholdi's statue was conceived as a gift from the French to the American people, intended to "glorify Liberty and the Republic, in the hope that these values will not die". Unveiled on October 28, 1886, the statue underwent a rejuvenating facelift before its 100th anniversary. Lady Liberty is a real giant: the statue proper weighs 221.5 tons and, including the base section, soars to a height of 305 feet. Leading from ground level to the crown (its seven rays representing the seven seas and seven continents) are 354 steps. A visit to the Statue of Liberty is a great way to start a tour of New York: from high up in the crown the whole city is spread out before you, and even the stunning skyscrapers appear dwarfed by her presence.

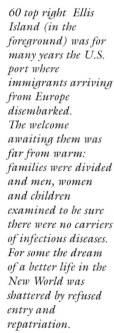

60 top right Ellis Island (in the foreground) was for many years the U.S. port where immigrants arriving from Europe disembarked. The welcome awaiting them was far from warm: families were divided and men, women and children examined to be sure there were no carriers of infectious diseases. For some the dream of a better life in the New World was shattered by refused entry and repatriation.

62 top Under a scintillating steel and glass roof is the most stunning area of the World Financial Center, the Winter Garden, a spacious, well-lit square decorated with tall palms.

62-63 The style of the twin towers of the World Trade Center aims to emphasise their dizzying height, enhanced by the seemingly infinite landscape of steel structures which also act as support to these airy, imposing buildings.

63 The World Financial Center, built exactly in front of the World Trade Center, is a complex formed by four glass and granite towers, two of which can be seen in the photograph.

Ellis Island and Lady Liberty are reached by ferry from Battery Park: this strip of green fringing the Hudson River was named after the line of cannons once set here to protect the city. You can still visit Castle Clinton. When it was built in 1807 it stood about 109 yards offshore but years of landfill have since connected it to the mainland. Battery Park is about the only real tract of greenery in the Financial District, better known as Wall Street. The wall in question was built by the Dutch colonists of New Amsterdam to mark the boundary between Indian territory and their own. Wall Street may now be synonymous with high finance but it is also custodian of some of New York's oldest memories, starting with Trinity Church, made particularly prominent by its tall Gothic bell tower. The present structure is the third church to stand on this site (the first was erected in 1697, making it one of the oldest Anglican churches in America); until 1860 it towered over the buildings all around. Federal Hall National Monument offers another historic testimony since this is the site where, in 1789, George Washington took his oath of office as first president of the United States. Although dwarfed by the surrounding skyscrapers, this neo-classical building is an imposing and fitting tribute, with a large statue of the president leading the way into an exhibition on the Constitution. Of no less significance are the Federal Reserve Bank, the U.S. government bank where there are vast strong-rooms crammed with gold, and the New York Stock Exchange, hub of global finance. We may have seen the NYSE in countless films but it is unlikely that anyone ignorant of the niceties of financial markets really understands its workings. Officially established in 1792 by a small group of brokers, it has been the scene of great stock market crashes (the most famous of all in 1929) and miraculous recoveries, respectively breaking

64 top From the visitors' balcony we can watch the feverish activity of the brokers and investors who crowd into the great hall of the New York Stock Exchange. A highly sophisticated telecommunications network and giant screens guarantee constant information on the financial movements of the world economy.

64-65 Seen from the Hudson River, from which there is easy access to the Winter Garden by a small jetty, the gigantic constructions of the World Financial Center seem almost tiny by comparison with the twin towers of the World Trade Center which rise up behind them.

or making investors in the space of hours. Now that computers appear to run the show, the frenzied activity on the trading floor seems to have lost some of its appeal. But the public can still watch the proceedings from a visitors' gallery as brokers and pages dash to and fro in the hope of making their clients' fortunes.

Also located in the Financial District are two of New York's most interesting urban developments. The World Financial Center, formed of four connected office towers, is much more than an office complex: it includes tens of shops and restaurants, a Winter Garden used for shows and cultural events and even a marina on the Hudson River. More traditional in both appearance and function, the twin towers of the World Trade Center still dominate the New York skyline. Practically at the summit of one of the towers is the Window on the World restaurant, more celebrated for its stunning views than for its food. And it takes a single ride in an elevator that whizzes you from ground to sky level in less than a minute to realize just how the world has changed since 1626, when Peter Minuit bought the island of Manhattan for 24 dollars' worth of trinkets.

65 top left Just a few steps away from Trinity Church, next to the Federal Hall National Monument, is a bronze statue which marks the very spot where George Washington took his oath of office as president of the United States, and celebrates this historic event.

65 top right Trinity Church was built in the Gothic style in 1846 on a site already occupied by two other churches in the past. The grand central nave of this Protestant parish church is supported by dual columns of carved pillars, which accentuate the vertical sweep.

65 bottom right One of the most familiar sights of the Big Apple seen from the air - the skyscrapers of Manhattan push upwards towards the sky, with the Empire State Building first in the race.

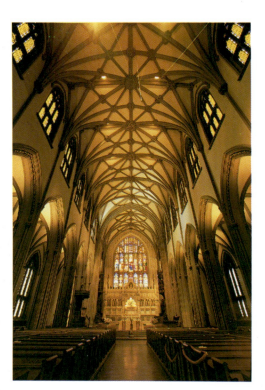

66 Inside the Federal Hall National Monument, the finest Neo-classical building of Lower Manhattan, the rotunda of marble columns stretches out, spacious and luminous, to welcome the visitors.

67/70 Skyscrapers is the term coined to describe these superb buildings, one of the many miracles the visitor to New York encounters, true triumphs of engineering in glass and steel, enabling man to climb to breath-taking heights.

71 The United States Custom House, built between 1834 and 1842, contains a number of rooms, such as the Alexander Hamilton room we see in the photograph. Several of these halls are used for exhibitions.

In the architecture of Lower Manhattan there is more than a hint of eclectism, with styles ranging from Art Deco to Renaissance, some buildings dating from the early twentieth century, others considerably older. Particularly worthy of note are the Downtown Athletic Club and the former U.S. Custom House, now home to a huge collection of American Indian art (about a million artifacts). Another prominent landmark is the Fraunces Tavern Museum, an exact replica of the tavern that witnessed several memorable episodes of the American Revolution. The southern banks of the Hudson may have the green edge but the shores of East River are now dominated by South Street Seaport. And this nineteenth-century "street of sails" has become one of the liveliest spots in town. In this long-neglected part of the city, the tide was turned by property developers who converted old warehouses and workshops into smart stores and trendy fish restaurants. The place to go for an insight into the area's maritime past is the South Street Seaport Museum but also not to be missed are Schermerhorn Row, with its magnificently restored Georgian-style warehouses, the historic ships docked alongside the piers, or a cruise on the *Andrew Fletcher* paddlewheeler. The Fulton Fish Market takes you back to the port's heyday when New York was the most important food trading centre of America. At the Maritime Craft Center you can watch woodcarvers busy creating magnificent model boats. And Pier 17 offers fine views of the famous Brooklyn Bridge. The story goes that an ingenuous but seriously rich tourist was once offered the Brooklyn Bridge for sale, and bought it... The world's first steel suspension bridge was constructed between 1869 and 1883 to a design by John A. Roebling, the engineer who built the bridge at Niagara Falls. Many new techniques were used in its construction. But the work claimed twenty lives, including Roebling's: he died from wounds caused by an on-site accident. His son Washington took over but decompression sickness eventually left him paralyzed and the task of supervising the project was passed on to his wife. Judging from the results, she made a good job of it.

73 top Bridges are an integral part of the New York landscape; some of them are masterpieces of construction and engineering. This aerial view shows East River crossed by the two southernmost bridges: Brooklyn Bridge and Manhattan Bridge.

74-75 In this spectacular photograph, Brooklyn Bridge reveals itself in all its symbolic, evocative power. This bridge is not only one of the most important communication routes between Manhattan and Brooklyn, but also an extraordinary, pioneering structure, halfway between myth and history.

72 and 73 bottom To explore the maritime and trading past of New York, nothing could be better than a visit to the South Street Seaport, and especially its Seaport Museum, which stretches for no less than eleven blocks along the seafront, and is made up of a complex of galleries, historic ships and craft workshops. One of the most fascinating aspects of a visit to the South Street Seaport is the chance to see these historic craft tied up in the harbour incorporated in the museum. And the contrast between the maritime past and the present, with its high office and residential buildings, is remarkable.

76-77 Chinese immigration has an almost constant element: the tendency to recreate a piece of their native country in their new homeland. Chinatown in New York is no exception: it is inhabited by more than 15,000 persons of Chinese origin and the Confucian or Buddhist temples – one of which is shown in this photograph – are among the fulcrums of Chinatown life.

77 top left Chinatown is in Lower East Side, where New York's multiethnic configuration is most in evidence. Canal Street marks the unofficial "border" between Chinatown and Little Italy.

77 top right It is said the Chinese are the world's best traders, capable, with a smile, of selling you just about anything. In Chinatown's maze of shops you'll find an astonishing product assortment, ranging from gingseng roots to the latest electronic gadgets. And the influence of Oriental architecture is eye-catching, even in the quarter's most modern buildings.

76 top This is New York, not Beijing - but you can get delicious Peking duck here every single day. Chinese communities are known worldwide for their cuisine. The Chinese restaurants of New York - serving the specialities of Canton, Szechuan and many other regions - are now far too many to be counted: accessible prices, as well as good food, are the key to their success.

76 bottom If all the proper ingredients for a real Chinese meal are wanted, a visit to Chinatown is the best solution. Oriental specialities galore can be bought here, as well as Western products.

In Lower East Side - on "this side" of Brooklyn Bridge - the immigrant heritage is still very much alive: entire neighbourhoods are still inhabited by children and grandchildren of Italians, Chinese, Jews from Eastern Europe who preserved the languages, customs and atmosphere of their homeland. There are no skyscrapers around these parts and cramped living conditions in the "railroad flats" (low-rise buildings with a high population density) creats an exceptionally lively street life. As you stroll from one block to the next it's like taking a rapid world tour. For the Jews on Orchard Street the "rag trade" is still the preferred line of business. They hope soon to see restoration of Eldridge Street Synagogue completed: this immense temple was built in 1887 by what eventually became the world's largest Jewish community. Nowadays shops displaying the menorah are flanked by others with distinctive paper lanterns, as Chinatown's traditional boundaries become too tight for its growing Asian community. Chinese immigrants now live all over New York but here they still breathe the atmosphere of "home" and these streets are packed during the noisy, colourful celebrations that mark the Chinese New Year. There is even a plaza dedicated to Confucius, and at the Wall of Democracy in Bayard Street you can read newspapers with reports on the political and social situation in China.

An equally bright and varied scenario is offered by Little Italy. The neighbourhood is known the world over for the festivities held for San Gennaro and Sant'Antonio of Padua, when immigrants from north and south of the Italian peninsula gather to pay tribute to their respective patron saints. Possibly only the very elderly recall the days when unsanitary conditions - together with promiscuity and lack of fresh air and sunshine - caused disease and death: situations that often strengthened immigrants' determination to escape and to forge their own "American dream". Films and books present a picturesque image of Italian Americans, sometimes portrayed as carefree spaghetti eaters and mandolin strummers, sometimes as dangerous mobsters whose watchword is omertà (the law of silence). Nowadays, Americans of Italian descent have achieved success in many fields (some outstanding examples being New Yorkers Martin Scorsese, Robert De Niro and Mario Cuomo) and Little Italy is packed with cafés and trattorias offering regional cuisine, patronised by those looking for a Mediterranenan atmosphere. Old St. Patrick's Cathedral (not to be confused with the one on Fifth Avenue) is the hub of the Italian community. Erected in the early 1800s (and rebuilt after destruction by fire in 1860), it is the oldest Roman Catholic church in the city. For a last taste of old New York in Lower East Side, make your way to Lafayette Street. A most unusual style was chosen for the old fire station still standing here (and now occupied by a cultural center): it was modelled on a Loire chateau, complete with dormers and towers.

78 left and 79
The feast-days of San Gennaro (left), at the end of September, and Sant'Antonio from Padua (right), in June, are always celebrated by the Italo-American community with a great get-together. For the first, Mulberry Street is closed to traffic and turned into a "little Naples", with illuminations, paraders holding aloft the saint's statue, and tables loaded with Italian food and drink. The cheerful spirit of earlier generations - on this occasion tinged with religious fervour - lives on in the general atmosphere and excitement.

78 top right
Even though the American Italians move and aspire towards integration into US society, we can often see extreme examples of their desire to keep in touch with their roots.

78 bottom right
According to Italo-American folklore, even though it reinforces their stereotype, this is what every Italian mamma should be like: cheerful, buxom and ready to serve up all sorts of tasty food.

80 top left Prince Street, which we catch a glimpse of in this photograph, is one of the most interesting streets in the SoHo area, the fashionable artists' quarter of the city.

80 bottom left The ultra-trendy buildings that add a blaze of colour to the SoHo area are all former warehouses or goods storehouses. Adopted by painters and other artists, their original appearance has been completely transformed.

80 top right and 81 top The graffiti of SoHo, first seen as a form of juvenile protest, are now an important medium of artistic expression. The decoration of subway carriages and street walls started in the mid-'80s in the Bronx but what are now considered works of art in their own right can be admired all over New York, just as in SoHo.

80-81 One of the opportunities the artists are offered in Soho, takes the form of displaying work to passers-by, hoping for a chance meeting with a gallery-owner or art collector.

Light years away are SoHo and newly re-developed TriBeCa. Both names are acronyms. SoHo - standing for South of Houston, in this case Houston Street - has been invaded in recent decades by artists, drawn by large attics and spacious lofts created from former warehouses. Encroaching skyscrapers were kept at bay thanks to conservationists' determination to save a rare architectural feature of the area's old buildings: façades created from cast-iron. Like other southern parts of Manhattan, SoHo has retained a lively atmosphere and a human scale. Some fine examples of cast-iron structures can be seen on Greene Street or West Broadway. To get an idea instead of the food mania that has recently gripped New Yorkers, a visit to Dean & DeLuca is de rigueur. In this enormous gourmet food store you'll find French baguettes and Italian coffee, at mind-boggling prices, as well as an incredible assortment of ready-to-serve dishes. For contemporary art buffs SoHo has numerous private galleries (Leo Castelli's, for instance), one of New York's newest museums (Guggenheim Museum SoHo, an offspring of the main Guggenheim Museum, designed by architect Arata Isozake), and a museum of African art. TriBeCa - from Triangle Below Canal - is really an extension of SoHo, literally as well as in spirit. It was formerly an industrial district and, earlier still, home to a farming community, which is somewhat hard to believe as your gaze takes in the many cast-iron structures and the plethora of trendy eateries, shops and galleries that now line the streets. A short way further north, continuing along the banks of the Hudson, is a quarter that has long been fashionable. Greenwich Village developed back in 1822, practically overnight, to cope with a sudden influx of city dwellers forced by a yellow fever epidemic to move out to what was then a rural settlement. Today it is one of the most delightful and vibrant parts of town. Its labyrinthine streets, in contrast with the prevailing grid plan, have always attracted artists, bohemians and all kinds of picturesque folk. Greenwich Village is really a world apart. Its population is predominantly young, on account of nearby New York University, founded in 1837 in Washington Square. An imposing arch by Stanford White domi-

82 St. Luke's Place in Greenwich Village is one of the loveliest streets in New York. Built in the mid-19th century, its beautiful Victorian-style houses seem untouched by the frenetic pace of the city. The street is also well-known for the poets and writers who have lived here.

nates this large open space (beware of whizzing frisbees: crossing the grass can sometimes be a risky undertaking). It was erected in the late nineteenth century to replace a wooden one that had marked the centenary of George Washington's inauguration as first president of the USA. A number of great writers and artists - Edith Wharton, Edward Hopper, e e cummings, Dos Passos - have lived close to the square. And while strolling around the Village streets, now dotted with bookstores and other tempting shops, you not infrequently notice beautiful old homes, reminders of the days when this was a quiet suburb. For instance, the lovely row of houses in St. Luke's Place, the tiny Bedford Street building where Cary Grant once lived (New York's narrowest home, about 3 yards wide), the gracious design of Grove Court. Another splendid building is the Jefferson Market Courthouse. This neo-Gothic castle-like structure, now converted to a public library, even has a fire lookout tower. East Village is also an enclave of artists and actors. Members of New York's high society once resided in this district but had vanished by the time waves of immigrants flooded in, early this century. Most notable among its landmarks are St.Mark's-in-the-Bowery Church - one-time chapel of the Stuyvesant family, rebuilt at the end of the 1700s - and the Public Theater. This red brick and brownstone building started life as a public library, funded by a bequest from the fur magnate Astor. Eventually, in 1966, it was bought by New York City as the home of the New York Shakespeare Festival. Albeit off-Broadway, the Public Theater has seen the debut of some famous musicals: for instance, *Hair*, furore-creating hit of the Sixties. Right opposite is Colonnade Row: in the gilded era of East Village the city's most prominent families lived in this once-grand edifice with its Corinthian columns. It now has little of its former splendour to show. Old Merchant's House, built in 1832, instead offers well-preserved traces of the very comfortable lifestyle of a wealthy hardware merchant, Seabury Tredwell, and his large family. East Village now pre-

83 top left Before housing the park which now offers the inhabitants of Greenwich Village a marvellous area of greenery, Washington Square was a swamp, then a cemetery.

83 bottom left Washington Square is a gathering point for the young, the New York University being very nearby. Chess, draughts, dominos, cards: concentration may not be helped by the suggestions of onlookers but it is still possible to enjoy a game in Washington Square.

83 top right In New York, it's literally impossible not to find made-to-measure entertainment. In the course of the year, hundreds of events of every conceivable type take place.

83 bottom right Houses and buildings in a full spectrum of lively colours help forge the style of the world's most famous metropolis.

84 top left The magic of New York isn't just in the outer shapes and colours of the buildings, but also in the surprise of magnificent interiors, such as this ceiling in the Conard Building.

84 bottom left The present building of the New York Public Library on Fifth Avenue dates back to 1897. The huge library houses some 18 million books: an immense treasure, accumulated partly thanks to collections contributed by benefactors like John Jacob Astor, Samuel Jones Tilden and James Lenox.

84 top right The photograph shows the East Room, one of the stupendous halls inside the Pierpont Morgan Library. The walls are decorated with murals showing historic figures, muses and signs of the zodiac. The library contains many old manuscripts and prints.

85 left The Flatiron Building, on the corner of Broadway and Fifth Avenue, is not only famous for its strange triangular shape. Built in 1902, it is also considered a forerunner of today's giant skyscrapers.

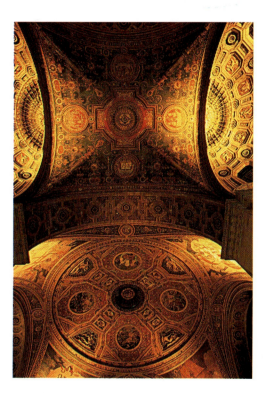

sents a very different picture, crowded with experimental music clubs, small off-Broadway theatres and heirs of the "beat generation", busy setting trends for global youth.

A totally different atmosphere exists around Gramercy Park, New York's only private park. Situated at the heart of an elegant and classy residential district, it is one of four squares (the others are Union, Stuyvesant and Madison) that were laid out around the mid-nineteenth century and represented something of a departure from typical urban development in the city. Gramercy Park, home to many Edith Wharton heroines, is an oasis of greenery for the sole enjoyment of the square's residents.

Visitors can admire these peaceful gardens and handsome buildings only through the wrought-iron gates. Union Square is more accessible, though definitely less exclusive. It is a popular place for political rallies and soapbox orators.

It marks the start of Ladies' Mile, a name coined in the nineteenth century when high-society ladies came here in their carriages to shop at fashionable stores like Lord & Taylor and Arnold Constable. Wedged into the triangle formed by Fifth Avenue, Broadway and 23rd Street is the Flatiron Building, after which this whole district is now named. Its unusual shape and exceptional height (until 1909 it was the world's tallest building) caused some anxious moments for its architect David Burnham.

Some people feared its days were numbered, predicting that winds created by its bold acute angle would cause its collapse. But the Flatiron is fortunately still standing and has even become a symbol of the city. It also marks the point where Chelsea "officially" begins. The hub of this district, which boasts many delightful nineteenth-century town houses, is Herald Square, named after the now-defunct *New York Herald* newspaper. Dominating the square - and much of the city - is the soaring Empire State Building.

A good place to start your visit to Chelsea is in the Garment District, along part of 7th Avenue. It has been the heart of the clothing industry since the 1930s, and has a workforce of around 200,000 in the city alone. Located right here is Macy's department store, a legendary name in the fashion world. In premises occupying an entire block, it sells just about everything, at every kind of price. Founded back in 1857, Macy's also sponsors the city's Thanksgiving Day parade along streets lined with enthusiastic New Yorkers, while at home the traditional roast turkey dinner awaits them.

Not surprisingly there are a number of long-established fashion and fabric design schools here. Also now a local institution is the Chelsea Hotel, a splendid example of cast-iron architecture. During its long life it has attracted well-known poets, writers and musicians.

85 top right Union Square is located at the point where Broadway meets Fourth Avenue, hence its name. In the years before World War I, it was the scene of demonstrations by socialists and anarchists; during the Depression the unemployed came here to voice their protests.

85 bottom right This highly original fountain with giraffes leaping around the sun, by Greg Wyatt, is in Gramercy Park, one of the most exclusive addresses in town.

86-87 Among the more or less recent skyscrapers of Manhattan, this view shows some of those which have caused the greatest stir with their daring, innovative architecture, such as the Woolworth Building, the Chrysler Building and the Empire State Building.

87 The Empire State Building, no longer the world's highest, is still the most famous skyscraper in New York, and perhaps the world. To scale its 449 metres, there are high speed lifts.

New York's quintessential symbol is the Empire State Building. Since King Kong climbed to its summit in 1933, it has been seen in countless movies set in the city. Admittedly, many other skyscrapers have joined it on the skyline since its inauguration in 1931 but this one, rising to a height of more than 1,420 feet, continues to attract the tourists. And not only tourists: lightning apparently strikes the mast above the observatory at least 500 times a year. During its still-brief history the Empire State Building has been the scene of many intriguing episodes (in 1945, for example, a military pilot confused by fog crashed his plane into the 78th

floor). The New York giant was an instant success: a 1939 guidebook claimed that, in the first five years, no fewer than 4 million people visited the observatories on the 86th and 102nd floors. Today it is reckoned the number must be around 85 million!

88 top The huge Madison Square Garden was built in 1968, after the lovely Pennsylvania Station had been bulldozed to make way for it. Able to seat 20,000 people, it provides a venue for big sport events, concerts, antiques shows and all kinds of exhibitions.

88-89 Times Square was once Longacre Square: it owes its present name to the New York Times which moved its offices here in 1904. The newspaper installed the world's first moving luminous sign in the square, starting a fashion that has been with us ever since.

89 top left At the heart of the Theatre District, Times Square offers entertainment for every kind of audience. The long queue of theatre-goers seen in this photo is waiting patiently at the kiosk where half-price tickets are sold.

89 top right Carnegie Hall is a terracotta and brick Italian Renaissance-style building. The acoustics of its concert hall are reckoned to be unrivalled worldwide.

89 right and centre The chaotic, speeding traffic around Times Square is unstoppable by day or night, with hundreds of cars and taxis rushing along the streets that contain the city's best known theatres.

As buildings go, Madison Square Garden also has its claim to fame. This concrete cylinder, used for major sports events and concerts, stands on the site once occupied by the lovely Pennsylvania Station. Its construction, deplored by aesthetes, gave way to a successful campaign by the city's intellectuals, to ensure the conservation of other historic buildings. We are now drawing close to the Theater District and Midtown, which together form the very heart of New York. The existence of a "theatreland" tells us a lot about New Yorkers' tastes. The theatres now scattered in abundance between Times Square and Columbus Circus started to open their doors in the nineteenth century, when the Metropolitan Opera House moved to Broadway. Movie houses eventually came, too - and went. But many survived and, with all the bright neon signs, Broadway became known as the "Great White Way". The enormous investments made to stage theatrical productions sometimes pay off and shows like the record-breaking *A Chorus Line* can run here for years. Hollywood screen stars who are household names gladly accept the challenge of performing for live audiences on Broadway. Certainly worth seeing, from the outside at least, is the Lyceum Theater, a charming Baroque-style structure erected in 1903 and miraculously saved from demolition at the end of the Thirties. Two other major sights in this district are the Shubert Theater and Carnegie Hall, which is considered to have among the best acoustics in the world. Carnegie Hall has welcomed outstanding conductors like Arturo Toscanini, Leopold Stokowski and Leonard Bernstein. It is now a national monument and meticulous renovation has restored its features to their former splendour. Broadway offers also a plethora of smaller playhouses where shows are not always an overnight success. Clustered around Times Square are numerous minor theatres where - for the performers - stardom is hard to achieve or short-lived. Around here you'll find many places for after-the-show wining and dining.

At the Russian Tea Room, for instance, you may be surprised to see an actor you had shortly before been admiring on-stage, seated at the next table. No-one can claim to have experienced the real "old New York" without savouring the ambience of the Algonquin Hotel. In the 1920s, New York literati associated with the *New Yorker* (still the most sophisticated magazine of the English-speaking world) gathered at the Round Table luncheon club, in the hotel's Rose Room; Dorothy Parker, Robert Benchley, Harold Ross and companions created some of the most memorable pages of American literature. Ladies convinced that "diamonds are a girl's best friend" should instead make for 47th Street, also known as Diamond Row. It is home to diamond traders (the majority are orthodox Jews who fled from Antwerp and Amsterdam before World War II).

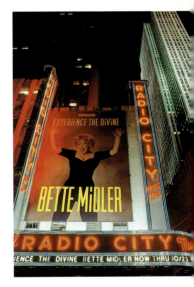

89 bottom right The lights of Radio City Music Hall, the massive auditorium within the Rockefeller Center, illuminate another New York night.

90 top and centre The Lower Plaza of the Rockefeller Center (above), a private complex unique of its kind, is an essential stopping point, perhaps for a drink under the brightly coloured umbrellas of the café.

The façades of the buildings and the open spaces are embellished by the works of more than 30 artists, such as the gigantic statue of Prometheus in front of the General Electric Building (centre).

90 bottom Among the buildings of the Rockefeller Center, which reached a total of 19 in 1973, is Building 636, whose façade decorated with this sculpture projects it onto Fifth Avenue.

90-91 One of the ideal moments to enjoy the atmosphere of the Rockefeller Center is during the Christmas holidays, a time to shop or walk around beneath the colourful, brightly lit Christmas tree.

Two sites in the Theater District sum up the importance New York attributes to patronage and the arts. The Rockefeller Center, officially declared a national landmark in 1985, is a vast complex embellished by the works of tens of artists. Its many buildings together form a city within the city, populated every day, for work or leisure, by hundreds of thousands of people. It now covers three blocks and comprises no fewer than 21 buildings linked by open space, walkways, shops and restaurants. Commissioned by John D Rockefeller, Jr., the design project was handled by a group of architects headed by Raymond Hood. The popularity of the complex is particularly evident in certain areas: everybody knows the ice rink - overlooked by a gilt statue of Prometheus - which in summer becomes a piazza dotted with the tables of an outdoor café; everybody has seen shows at Radio City Music Hall; and sipping an evening cocktail while admiring the urban panorama from the Rainbow Room can be a stirring experience. The second site is the immense New York Public Library, occupying two whole blocks on Fifth Avenue. Preserved under the watchful gaze of Patience and Fortitude (two stone lions named by New York's now legendary mayor, Fiorello La Guardia) are some 20 million volumes, plus some 10,000 current periodicals from every corner of the globe. The library is also proud owner of original manuscripts of many famous literary works, and a Gutenberg Bible.

91 top left Lee Lawrie, with his many works, is one of the artists most on view in the Rockefeller Center. One of his finest works is "Wisdom", which we can admire on the G. E. Building.

91 top right Liberty is one of the dominant styles in the group of works that adorns the buildings of the Rockefeller Center.

Extending eastwards on the other side of Fifth Avenue is the realm of skyscrapers. Many of these symbols of modernity were built in the Art Deco period and their decorative features point to an eclectic mix of styles and taste.

A sensible place to start a tour of the area is its only 'low-rise' sight: Grand Central Terminal, a huge Beaux Arts railway station built from marble and granite. Its details are no less stunning than its vast proportions: the clock above the main entrance, set among sculptures of Greek deities, the flights of steps emulating the staircase in the Paris Opera House, the vaulted ceiling of the concourse, with its designs of the constellations. But perhaps most impressive of all are the crowds of people that rush to and fro at every hour of day and night, so dissimilar from those who passed through this terminal a century ago, when a train journey was looked upon as a great adventure, to be related in every detail to wide-eyed grandchildren.

92-93 How many railway stations can boast regular tours organized for tourists? Grand Central Terminal is one of them. Above the main entrance, on 42nd Street, is a clock topped by sculptures of allegorical figures.

93 bottom The construction of the Pan Am (now MetLife) Building in 1963 triggered vociferous protests and debates on account of its huge size. The roof was used as a heliport until about 20 years ago, when it was closed for safety reasons.

93 top This unusual four-faced clock can be found in the foyer of the Grand Central Terminal, right above the kiosk housing the information office.

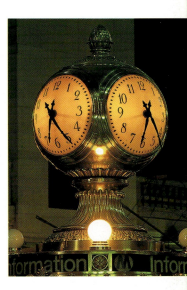

94 top left The headquarters of the United Nations Organisation looks onto the East River in Lower Midtown. Even though it is located in the heart of New York, the area isn't part of United States territory, as it is technically an international zone.

94 centre left The current headquarters of the United Nations dates back to the Fifties and John Rockefeller Jr. made a financial contribution to its construction. The complex is adorned with many works of art - in this photograph, we can see the Statue of Peace.

Only a few steps away is the 1930 Chrysler Building, commissioned by Walter Chrysler. Its distinctive profile features a series of "crowns" topped with a spire. Chrysler's dream - that it should be the world's tallest building - faded within months with the completion of the Empire State Building. But this skyscraper remains a landmark on the New York skyline, now crowded with anonymous structures like the MetLife Building (formerly known as the Pan Am Building). Other more interesting sights include the Helmsley Building, on Park Avenue: its owners, Harry Helmsley and his extravagant wife Leona, were among the most prominent figures of New York's beau monde in the Eighties. Another exceptional place to visit is the Pierpont Morgan Library, built to house banker J. Pierpont Morgan's private collection and now custodian of outstanding collections of rare books, manuscripts and prints. Standing on the banks of East River are the United Nations headquarters, built thanks to a donation from John D. Rockefeller, Jr. The land it stands on is in fact not U.S. territory but an international zone, a state within the city. Visitors on guided tours of the complex have a chance to admire many works of art that adorn the buildings and gardens. The best known of all is a bronze statue by Eugeny Vuchetich, inscribed with the words of Isaiah, "They shall beat their swords into plowshares, and their spears into pruning forks: nation shall not lift up sword against nation, neither shall they learn war any more".

94 bottom left The distinctive spire of the Chrysler Building, with its Art Deco arched structures, stands out in the background alongside one of the UNO headquarters buildings.

94 right This photograph shows an unusual overlap of Manhattan skyscrapers standing out against a crystal clear sky, in an interplay of glass and steel.

95 The Chrysler Building is a shrine to the founder of the great car manufacturing company, and its products. The crowning spire, in stainless steel, recalls the grid of a car radiator, while other parts of the structure echo different car components. With its 77 floors it is by no means the city's tallest building, but it remains an outstanding landmark.

96 top The Gothic revival façade of Saint Patrick's Catholic Cathedral is mirrored on the glass of the buildings which almost hide it.

In Upper Midtown, only blocks away from the place where representatives of nations work to maintain world peace, a very different "battle" is in progress. This time the contestants are Fifth Avenue's smartest boutiques, its most luxurious hotels, the limousines that sweep past the taxis of common mortals. Here we can observe what non-New Yorkers perceive to be the very essence of the city, as immortalized on screen and described by Tom Wolfe with wry humour in *The Bonfire of the Vanities*. In the heart of this district is St.Patrick's Cathedral, the largest Catholic church in America, a triumph of Gothic spires, chapels and stained-glass windows. Nearby is another "temple", the Waldorf-Astoria: this magnificent hotel in Art Deco style has always had the honour of hosting the U.S. presidents during visits to the country's "moral capital". And completing a unique trio of typical New York styles is the Seagram Building, designed by the brilliant Dutch architect Mies van der Rohe. His combined use of bronze and glass has created a structure flooded with light and, especially when you cast your eyes from base to summit, the building appears to thrust upwards almost weightless. Anyone intrigued by the fickle world of New York's beau monde will want at least to see the atrium of the Trump Tower, built by the most talked-about businessman of the Eighties, Donald Trump. His showpiece exudes opulence and special ef-

96-97 and 97 top right On ever-fashionable Fifth Avenue is the sumptuous Trump Tower, offering offices and apartments for the really well-heeled. Almost as famous are the stores in its glitzy atrium, a flamboyant ensemble of marble, glass and gilt finishings.

97 bottom right The Chrysler Building, alongside other skyscrapers, is reflected in an impressive photograph which amplifies the dizzying sensation created by these imposing buildings.

fects splurged with a prodigality no Spielberg film could rival. If the name Audrey Hepburn still arouses feelings of nostalgia (or you have read Truman Capote's book), a pilgrimage to Tiffany's is not to be missed. The store's old-world elegance and delightfully helpful sales staff are as legendary as the precious jewels it sells. Other names emerging from the past include Bloomingdale's and the huge Plaza Hotel: proclaimed the world's best when it opened in 1907, it has recently undergone thorough refurbishment.

99 left The long ribbon of Fifth Avenue, punctuated here and there by the bright yellow of taxis, is the classic promenade for the shopping among the most luxurious shops in town.

98 top left and right You can go the length of Fifth Avenue in a taxi, in a limousine, by subway, even on foot provided you go shopping. Whether you call in at Tiffany & Co.,

Bulgari, Bergdorf Goodman, Saks, Gucci, Christian Dior, Elizabeth Arden or any other store on the street, you'll find only the best of luxury goods on sale.

98 bottom left Lee Lawrie's Atlas, lit up by night lights, soars majestically upwards at the entrance to the International Building, one of the buildings on the outer periphery of the Rockefeller Center.

99 right Overlooking Fifth Avenue is St.Patrick's Cathedral, the largest Roman Catholic church in America, built in Gothic Revival style. It was consecrated on May 25, 1879. At the time the choice of site met with some criticism: it was then on the outskirts of the city nucleus.

100

100 top Skating beneath the impassive expression of Lawrie's Prometheus is one of the favourite pastimes in the Rockefeller Center. Here we see a splendid foreground shot of the statue's fiery hand upraised.

100-101 The imposing statue, white from a recent snowfall, is of General Sherman, and stands out against one of the luxurious buildings of the Grand Army Plaza.

101 top In this winter view of Central Park, we can see skaters relaxing and enjoying the fun in the Wollman Rink, far from the bustle of the city, as symbolised by the skyscrapers in the background.

101 bottom The Empire State Building emerges shrouded in mystery between the mist and the snow in an almost magical atmosphere. The New York landscape is unique and unmistakable even when surrounded by the drapes of winter.

102 Les Demoiselles d'Avignon - *apart from* Guernica *which is housed in Madrid - is probably the best known of Pablo Picasso's works. Even more than 90 years on (it was painted in 1907) it has not lost its transgressive force. Of course, clusters of visitors to the Museum of Modern Art constantly gather in front of the painting.*

*103 top left
The photograph shows the main entrance to the Museum of Modern Art (more commonly known as MOMA), New York's shrine of modern art. Besides collections of contemporary paintings and sculptures, from Cézanne to the present day, the museum has a section dedicated to industrial design.*

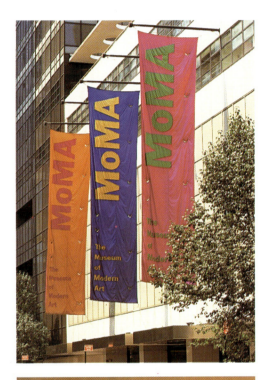

After so much glitz and glamour, the Museum of Modern Art offers welcome visual and intellectual relief. This splendid collection of contemporary art is housed in a structure both varied and vibrant. Visitors interested not just in paintings can sit or stroll in the Sculpture Garden. And once inside the now-hallowed walls they can feast their eyes on countless masterpieces, among them Picasso's *Les Demoiselles d'Avignon*, Van Gogh's *The Starry Night* and *Monet's Water Lilies*.

The MOMA is known and appreciated for its broader approach to artistic disciplines (with emphasis on industrial design and architecture) and is considered at the cutting edge of twentieth century art.

If, before leaving Upper Midtown, you take a leisurely walk down to the East River, film-goers may well recognize a now-famous spot: the bench below Queensboro Bridge on which Woody Allen and Diane Keaton fell in love in *Manhattan*.

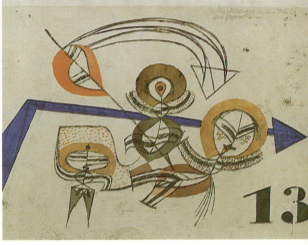

*103 bottom left
The picture shows Marilyn in Gold, one of Andy Warhol's works. The artist has always been linked with Pop Art, and his approach to art is well summarized in his famous remark: "In the future everyone will be famous for fifteen minutes".*

*103 top right
The colours of Provence explode even in this "nightly" work by Vincent Van Gogh, the most celebrated* Starry Night. *Bursting stars illuminate the sky, interrupted by the tall shadow of cypresses. This work is a painting no visitor to MOMA should miss.*

*103 bottom right
The list of famous names encountered on MOMA's walls is endless. But Paul Klee's works alone would justify a trip to New York. Instantly recognizable is his* Playing with Thirteen, *shown here.*

104 top Opening the Greek and Roman art collections is a monumental kouros; the very first contribution to this section was a donated Roman sarcophagus from Tarsus. Of particular interest is an exhibition of precious Roman glasswares.

104 bottom Keen interest in the art of ancient Egypt led to many expeditions organized ad hoc to increase the collections of "The Met".

104-105 The original project for the Met's current site was by Calvert Vaux and J. Wrey Mould, but the building has since been extended and restructured. The main section in "Roman" style, opened in 1902, was designed by Richard Morris Hunt and his son, Richard Howland.

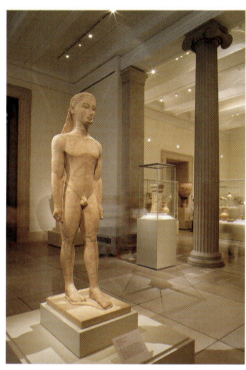

East of Central Park is Museum Mile, where most of the city's public art galleries and museums are located. Upper East Side is also a smart residential district and a plethora of upmarket stores line Park Avenue and Madison. To walk the length of Fifth Avenue, stopping to spend only an hour or two in each museum, would take you... at least a week! Undisputed star of the scenario, right on the park, is the Metropolitan Museum of Art. Even the most bizarre and eclectic tastes will be satisfied by its myriad collections: from the Temple of Dendur, now enclosed in a huge glass-house, to Van Gogh; from the "chinoiserie" of the Astor Court to the Flemish masters; from pre-Columbian carved masks to Edward Hopper.

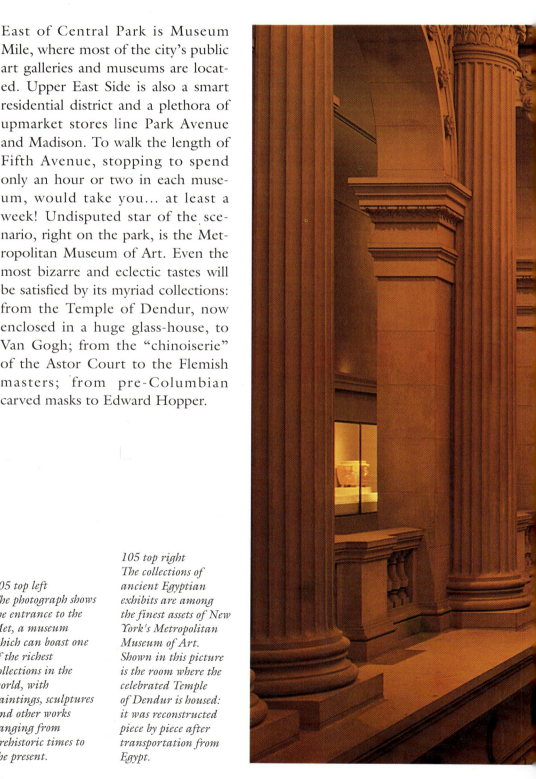

105 top left The photograph shows the entrance to the Met, a museum which can boast one of the richest collections in the world, with paintings, sculptures and other works ranging from prehistoric times to the present.

105 top right The collections of ancient Egyptian exhibits are among the finest assets of New York's Metropolitan Museum of Art. Shown in this picture is the room where the celebrated Temple of Dendur is housed: it was reconstructed piece by piece after transportation from Egypt.

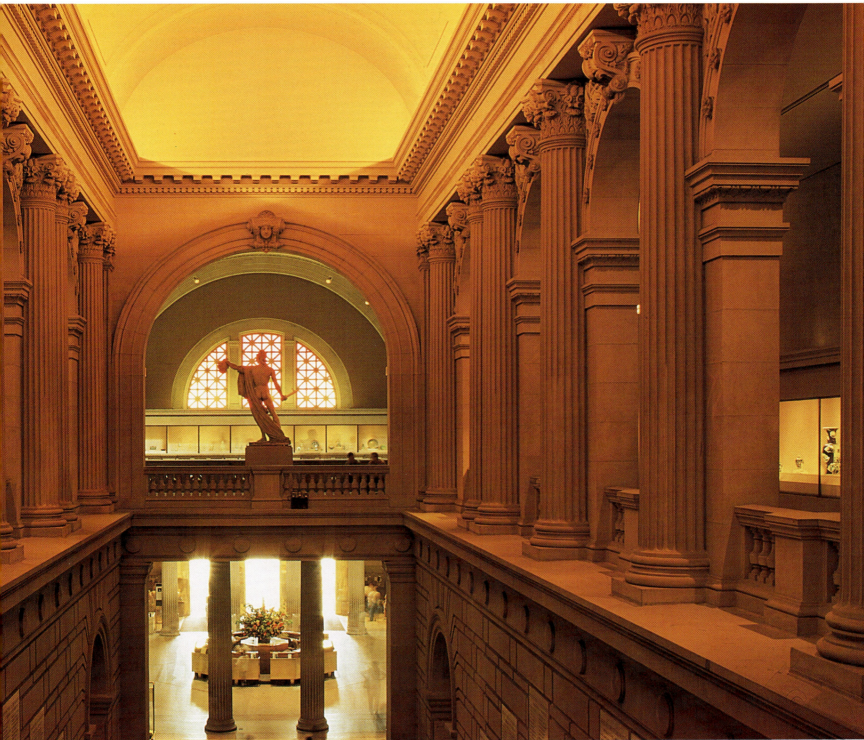

106 top left Game of Cards *is one of the 17 works of Cézanne housed in the Met. The peasants engrossed in their game were painted by the artist in 1890.*

106 top right The image shows Paul Klee's Arab town scene, *painted in 1923: like Kandisky, Klee was associated with the Blaue Reiter artists and the formative experience at the famous Bauhaus.*

106-107 The unmistakable Répétition d'un Ballet sur Scene *by Edgar Degas was painted in 1873-74. Female dancers, seen together with café-concert singers and jockeys, were one of the French painter's favourite subjects for a time.*

107 top One of the pictures from Paul Gauguin's Tahitian period shows two native girls, a subject which always captured his attention when far from frenetic Paris life.

107 bottom It could be said that Impressionism stemmed from the close association between Monet and Renoir. From Auguste Renoir's more mature period comes this splendid example of landscape painting: a view of the coast near Wargemont, in Normandy.

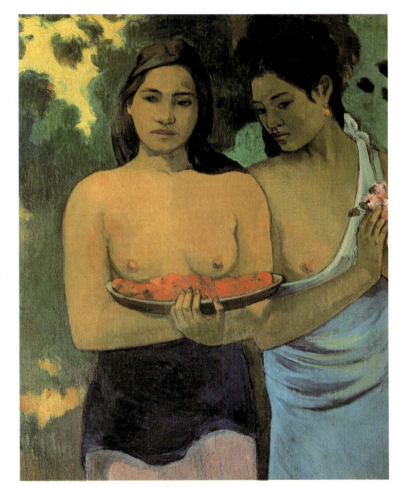

108 top left Joan Miró, the Catalan artist of the butterflies and the moon, created incomparable mythical figures with a lightness of touch, as we can see in this work from 1927.

108 top right In this painting from 1911, The Drinking Soldier, the Russian visionary Marc Chagall offers a highly personal interpretation of the everyday object, at the outer limits of reality in both form and colour.

108-109 and 109 top left Every conceivable space in New York's Solomon Guggenheim Museum was designed around its main purpose - the enhancement of the works of art it was to house, leading the visitor in a journey of mind and spirit. Solomon Guggenheim, a millionaire and lover of modern art, built up a significant collection of works by Kandinsky, Chagall, Léger and Delaunay. He called in the greatest contemporary American architect, Frank Lloyd Wright, to create the spaces needed to house his collection, and the result was a structure that just can't go unnoticed.

109 bottom left Amedeo Modigliani, with his Young Man in a Blue Jacket, *painted in 1918, is one of the many artists with works in the "Big Seashell", the Guggenheim, which faces onto Fifth Avenue.*

109 right Roy Lichtenstein, one of the most important representatives of American Pop Art, took his inspiration from the world of advertising and strip cartoons. Preparedness, *shown here, is one of the most significant works by Lichtenstein.*

Further along Fifth Avenue your gaze will be drawn to the huge spiral structure conceived by Frank Lloyd Wright as the home of the Solomon Guggenheim Museum, named after a family celebrated for its patronage of the arts.
Special and visiting exhibitions are mounted in the Great Rotunda whereas the permanent collections are displayed in the Tower galleries.

To list all the artists whose work can be seen here would be an enormous task. Suffice it to say that the museum has many prized possessions, with works by artists such as Kandinsky and Picasso.

110 top left The photograph shows the grandiose building in Georgian style which houses the New York City Museum, seen through the branches of the trees in Central Park.

110 bottom left The museum also offers stirring tributes to great New Yorkers of the past, like this room dedicated to actor John Barrymore.

110 top right The foundation stone of the present complex occupied by the American Museum of Natural History - set up thanks to the financial support of private benefactors - was laid by President Grant in 1874. Its rooms were opened to the public three years later. Throughout the institution's existence leading naturalists have contributed to its exhibits.

On Central Park West you'll find the American Museum of Natural History, the largest natural history museum in the world. It would take days to make a thorough tour of this monument to natural science but it can be a great place to spend Sundays with children, who will stare in amazement at its life-like reproductions of natural environments, dinosaur skeletons soaring ceiling-wards in spacious Victorian rooms, a section of a giant sequoia and numerous interactive exhibitions. Not far from here stands the

complex of the Hayden Planetarium, but New York has numerous museums with equally important collections: the Jewish Museum, the Cooper-Hewitt Museum, the International Center of Photography (more often called the ICP, founded by the brother of the outstanding photojournalist, Robert Capa), the Frick Collection, the National Academy of Design, the Whitney Museum of American Art and the delightful Museum of the City of New York. The list goes on and on...

110 bottom right The huge African elephants are one of the main attractions of the American Museum of Natural History, with notable appeal to both adults and the youngest visitors.

111 left A mother brontosaurus attempts to protect her "little one" from an attacking predator: a scene that amazes and moves every visitor to the American Museum of Natural History, the world's biggest natural history museum.

111 right The bright, spacious hall of the City of New York Museum contains two scale models of the Empire State Building, one of the symbols of the city.

112 top The green arm of Central Park stretches beyond the skyscrapers of Manhattan, a true oasis of peace and quiet in the heart of the city.

112-113 Bow Bridge, an arch reaching over the enormous Central Park Lake, links a densely wooded area, The Ramble, with Cherry Hill.

113 top Central Park extends from Central Park South to Central Park North, corresponding to 59th and 110th Streets. The park offers New Yorkers and visitors a wonderful place to relax and "let off steam". And what better way to forget the congested traffic and frenzied pace of life all around than a romantic drive in a carriage...

113 centre The project for Central Park, signed by Frederick Law Olmsted and Calvert Vaux, involved not only moving huge quantities of earth and rocks, but also creating a landscape featuring bridges, ponds and scenic footpaths. Over the years the area has acquired further assets: sites that encourage relaxation, sports facilities, cycle paths, and a skating rink.

113 bottom Although so different in character, Manhattan and Central Park are indivisible. The city desperately needs this vast green space, just as the natural beauty of the park would not be as prized without the juxtaposition of brick, steel, glass and concrete.

After this feast of art and culture, a walk in Central Park - verdant heart of New York - is a tempting proposition. This much loved and extremely popular place is wonderful in summer when the shade of half a million trees offers respite from the torrid heat of the city streets, but is just as delightful in "Fall" when ablaze with red foliage. Its manmade lakes and hills, arched bridges and pathways ideal for joggers are familiar to whole generations of young New Yorkers, who come here to learn about trees and plants, to make the acquaintance of animals at the Wildlife Conservation Center and to sail their model boats on Conservatory Water. The Dairy was once a small farm whose fresh milk helped put some red into the cheeks of pale city kids. Today this little Gothic-style building is the park information centre, where maps and details about events can be obtained. In summer Central Park provides the venue for important concerts and theatrical performances (like the celebrated "Shakespeare in the Park"). But here entertainment comes in many forms: watching people playing frisbee, listening to preachers or storytellers, or feeding the countless squirrels in search of nuts.

114-115 Crowned by the spires of Manhattan's most surprising skyscrapers, Central Park stretches out beneath a warm twilight sky.

116 The Low Library of Columbia University, one of the USA's oldest universities, is seen here from the main courtyard. The Alma Mater Statue stands halfway up the entrance stairway.

116-117 Not far from Columbus Circus is the Lincoln Center for the Performing Arts, which can be the stage for the most varied forms of show. The complex was built at the end of the Fifties in a run-down part of town (the slums that inspired Leonard Bernstein's musical West Side Story) and includes the Metropolitan Opera House, New York State Theater, Avery Fisher Hall and Alice Tully Hall.

117 top The Cathedral of St. John the Divine appears destined never to reach completion. Construction work started long ago in 1892 but the methods employed, reflecting medieval building techniques wherever possible, have made progress incredibly slow. Nevertheless, with its lovely chapels, portals, rose window, carved pillars and delightful garden, the cathedral is like a haven that has lost all connection with time.

Upper West Side also has some important attractions for music and drama lovers. Most prominent of all is the Lincoln Center which has concert-halls, theatres and also incorporates "The Met", the great Metropolitan Opera House. A further spectacle - for free - is offered by architecture in the surrounding streets. Several buildings in Upper West Side have made a notable impact on the city landscape, particularly the Twin Towers of Central Park West and the Dakota, a splendid luxury apartment building, known also as the site of the murder of its most famous resident, John Lennon. For unshakeable Beatles fans, almost opposite in the park is Strawberry Fields, a tribute to the great musician funded by his widow Yoko Ono. Situated beyond the line-up of high-rise buildings is another park, Riverside, with views over the Hudson. This area was developed towards the end of the 1800s and its buildings reflect the overstated eclectic taste of the wealthy families who chose to make their home here. A totally different world lies on the other side of Central Park. The first evidence of the transformation is Columbia University campus, imbued with an atmosphere that spreads the length of Amsterdam Avenue. Here the scenario is dominated by students, seen in huddles in local cafés talking passionately of poetry and revolution. America's most sought-after literary award, the Pulitzer Prize, was created in Columbia's School of Journalism, and some fifty Nobel prize-winners have been among many outstanding alumni who once studied in the splendid Butler Library (the presence of a student body of only 20,000 or so in a complex of these dimensions points to rigorous selection procedures prior to admission). Not far from the Columbia campus is the Cathedral of St. John the Divine, an immense structure that seems never to reach completion. There is a good reason for this. Despite America's passion for advanced technology, medieval construction methods are being used to build this Romanesque-style cathedral. Its capitals may be adorned with carved re-creations of New York skyscrapers but growing in the small garden is every single variety of plant named in the Bible, and the techniques employed in Stonemasons' Yard are all of eight hundred years old.

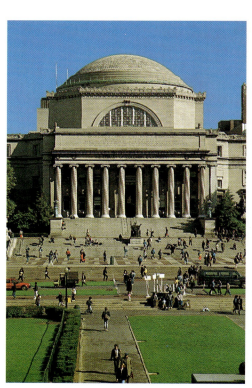

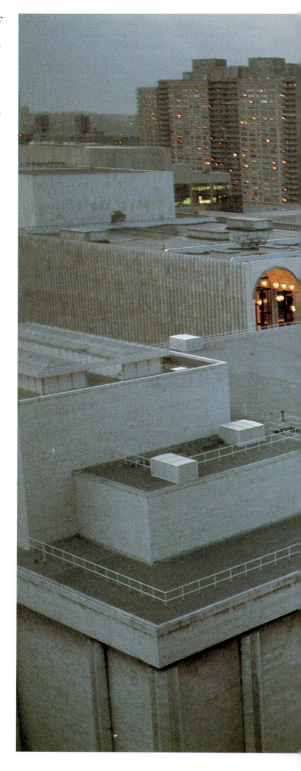

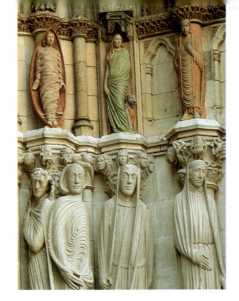
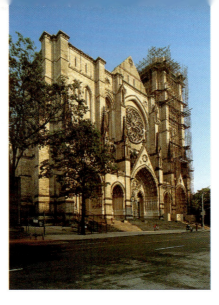

118 top Harlem is almost synonymous with the Afro-American community. The old houses in Lenox Avenue (now called Malcolm X Avenue) take us back to the glorious era of jazz and swing, when music aficionados had a fixed rendezvous at the Apollo Theater, where talents such as those of Duke Ellington and Billy Holiday were displayed.

118-119 Built in the late 19th century, the houses in St. Nicholas District adhere to a fixed model but incorporate an element of variety; although designed by different architects, they form a balanced, harmonious group.

Only a few blocks away is the boundary between Manhattan and Harlem, one of America's biggest black communities. Back in the Twenties Harlem saw the birth of the swing era, bringing jazz and blues that have influenced music for the rest of the twentieth century. A particularly celebrated night-spot was the Cotton Club (still in operation, on a more modest scale) where Cab Calloway and Duke Ellington used to perform. In those years New York intellectuals came to Harlem to hear the big bands play. Today tourists come to see the sights especially on Sunday mornings when they can listen to gospel choirs in the local churches. They end their visit with an African-American style brunch, with plenty of southern-fried chicken and sweet potato pie. After moments of alarming social and racial tension, Harlem's black community is now attempting to present the neighbourhood in a new light. For this district too has several museums well worth visiting: for instance, the Museo del Barrio, a tribute to the Latin-American community; the Studio Museum, with collections exemplifying African-American culture; and above all, the Schomburg Center for Research into Black Culture, a vibrant cultural centre with an exceptionally well-endowed library. We know New York is not just Manhattan. We also know that few visitors venture beyond the island's "pillars of Hercules". But to really get to know the city, a number of other sights should be on the itinerary of any self-respecting tourist. We have chosen three representative aspects of this fascinating melting pot of races and cultures. The first sight on this briefest of tours is the Cloisters. A museum of medieval art in the New World might seem an anachronism. And in effect, all the pieces gathered together in this complex in Washington Heights, northeast of Manhattan, originated in the Old Continent. They were brought here from Europe by American artist George Barnard, and assembled thanks to a generous donation from John D. Rockefeller, Jr. "Imported" from France and Spain and reconstructed stone by stone, the Cloisters hosts examples of Romanesque and Gothic art, tapestries, statuary and precious religious artifacts. Although it may seem out of place on U.S. soil, the Cloisters complex is an excellent example of America's ability to appreciate and preserve man's finest artistic creations. We have no wish to point accusing fingers but we doubt whether, had these masterpieces remained in their native lands, they would have been similarly cherished.

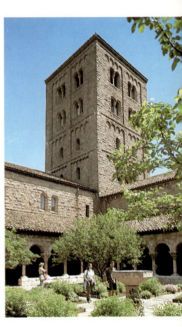

119 p A group of boys plays basketball near Lenox Avenue, perhaps hoping to follow in the footsteps of leading American basketball champions. The background shows a mural painting of New York skyscrapers.

119 bottom The Cloisters, a step back in time, a few minutes away from the futuristic skyscrapers of Manhattan. The building was constructed in the 1930's to contain in suitable surroundings an impressive collection of medieval antiques collected by George Barnard. As well as the collections, it is interesting to admire how the atmosphere of a European monastery has been reconstructed.

120 top The Hudson River, one of the city's most important navigable waterways, owes its name to the explorer Henry Hudson.

120-121 Brooklyn seen from Seaport. Two of the most outstanding parts of this huge area are Park Slope and Brooklyn Heights.

Our second stop - on the other side of the world's most famous bridge - is in Brooklyn, itself a huge city where races and cultures mix but don't easily mingle. Several residential districts, like Brooklyn Heights, merit a visit, as does the Brooklyn Museum. But if you want to keep the kids amused, go to the Children's Museum, prototype of thousands of similar institutions scattered the world over. Here "hands-on" is the key word: in this interactive environment geared to the younger generation the fine dividing line between play and learning totally disappears.

You'll find fun for all the family on Coney Island, our third and last port of call, a giant playground where you can stroll along Atlantic beaches or take your pick of hair-raising roller coaster rides. Admittedly many of the simple pleasures enjoyed by early twentieth-century daytrippers pale beside the hi-tech wonders of Disney parks. But people still recall the hard years of the Depression when, with a couple of cents spent on Coney Island, poverty and anguish were momentarily banished, and even destitute city dwellers could, like Roosevelt, dream of a better, fairer world.

121 top Brooklyn - on the other side of the famous bridge - would qualify as the fourth largest city in the United States were it not now a borough of New York. A bench along the East River promenade is a fine vantage point from which to gaze in wonder at the spectacular cityscape of Manhattan.

121 bottom Brooklyn and Manhattan Bridges link the main island of New York to Brooklyn, a zone that joined forces with Manhattan around a century ago. Before this, it had been a separate city, the third largest in the United States.

122 top left A team of workmen photographed during maintenance work on the Brooklyn Bridge.

122 bottom left Williamsburg, in North Brooklyn, created at the start of the 19th century by Colonel Williams, hosts one of the largest Hassidic communities in the world.

THE BEAT OF THE "BIG APPLE"

Could it be that in New York they've discovered the secret of perpetual motion? It's not only taxis, limousines, subway trains, buses, pedestrians and kids on skates that are constantly on the move, rushing from Harlem to Wall Street, from the Theater District to Soho, from Brooklyn to the Cloisters. The city itself changes face from one day to the next. Time and again a run-down district considered good for little besides demolition, suddenly becomes the fashionable place to live and a new real estate boom is triggered.

One such mystery is the success of TriBeCa, an old industrial area upgraded to artists' colony, after the conversion of warehouses and workshops into stylish lofts, galleries and smart restaurants.

A similar invasion by painters, sculptors, actors and the like has transformed Williamsburg, a former working-class part of Brooklyn. Keeping in step with the trend, the Harlem Urban Development Corporation is busy restructuring and refurbishing property, as a new wave of Spanish-speaking immigrants changes the appearance of the city's most famous black quarter. New York on the move is a city where everything becomes possible, provided you learn to live at a pace that outstrips other cities of America, let alone Europe. And yet even this seething metropolis affords frequent reminders of another, almost forgotten world:

122 top right 42nd Street is no ordinary thoroughfare - it's the Theater Row. The street is legendary for its lively atmosphere, not only by night, when the fans of musical and comedy pour in this district, but also during the day.

122 centre right A colourful new view of Times Square, one of the areas in which you need only walk around the streets to enjoy the theatre experience.

122 bottom right New York's firemen are very popular. At the origins of the city's history, fire was one of the most difficult enemies to fight. The worst fire was probably the one that broke out in 1776 where the Financial District is currently situated.

123 There's nothing unusual about a scene like this in New York - open-air chess offers a chance to make new friends and match your skills with those of constantly changing opponents.

124 The Hard Rock Café, with the typical period automobile built in above the entrance, is one of a successful chain of nightspots opened in Los Angeles and now spread throughout the world.

125 left The Harley Davidson Café is designed for the lovers of America's best known form of two-wheeled transport, which continues to act out a mythical role for more than one generation.

125 top right Just like in Paris, New York has many "oyster bars", where you can enjoy fresh shellfish and good chilled wine.

Orthodox Jews with their black hats, skullcaps and long locks of hair, chattering in Yiddish; high-society ladies elegantly attired in suit, hat and handbag, who sit sipping tea; children in school uniform queueing two-by-two outside a museum.

Here, where a skyscraper can disappear practically overnight to be replaced by another in the space of months, old-established luxury hotels do their best to preserve a precious architectural heritage: the Plaza, for instance, since 1986 a National Landmark, or the Waldorf Astoria with its meticulously executed Art Deco ornamentation. Among the newer-comers, the Paramount (near Times Square) conceived by Philippe Starck (one of the leading figures of 20th-century design) extremely rich in original details, like roses "planted" in marble and changed daily.

There's nothing money can't buy here, but even a multi-millionnaire will find life hard-going if he fails to enter into the spirit of New York. You have to be ready to adapt, to "go with the flow" in a city that makes itself seen and heard at every moment of the day.

New York is heard in the seemingly never-abating roar of traffic, in the sirens of police cars and fire-engines, in the thousands of different languages that fill your ears on the sidewalk. It is seen as soon as you walk out of your home or hotel, in the steam rising from manhole covers and in young go-getters who grab a sandwich at a street corner before dashing back to business. It is seen in perennial queues: for a successful movie or to get a cheap ticket for the theatre, or to enter a museum where a special exhibition is on. New York is career girls wearing beautifully tailored suits and trainers, with their stiletto heels tucked into a bag, ready to slip on outside the office door. It is the restaurants - Chinese, Vietnamese, Thai, Mexican, Italian, Hungarian - where you get a marvellous meal for a few dollars, but need your own "take-in" wine. It is huge slices of pizza covered with layers of melting

125 centre right New York is a city of limitless resources and opportunities. Going out at night is no problem, you'll always find the spot you're looking for. Ballagheri's, for example, offers a calm, relaxed atmosphere.

125 bottom right The photograph shows one of the most trendsetting clothing stores for the young, the famous Levi's Store, which boasts imitations throughout Europe.

126 top Broadway is an infinite parade of theatres, where the top productions take to the stage to obtain the definitive accolades of success.

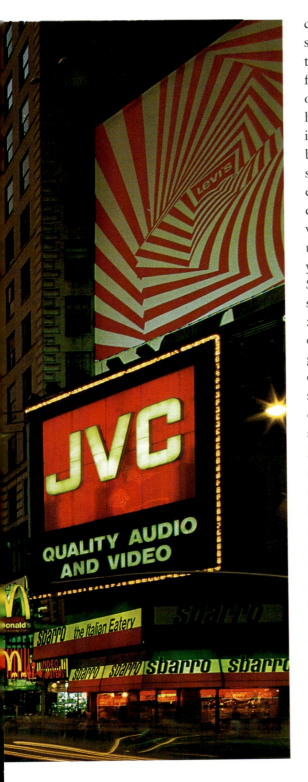

cheese, pepper and sausage, blinis served with caviar and Smetana at the Russian Tea Room, the "soul" food dished up at Sylvia's in Harlem or the sushi-sashimi-tempura that has practically ousted the hotdog. It is sidewalks lined with designer boutiques and luxury department stores, whole areas given over to electronics, musical instruments or even diamonds, stalls where street vendors offer "white elephants" at unbeatable prices (with a bit of luck you might take home a Fifties or Sixties gem for a song...). It is tiny stores and shopping malls, giant-sized hamburgers and gastronomic delights from every corner of the globe. It is avant-garde galleries and outrageously original shows, museums packed with old masters and contemporary art, "outdoor museums" in the form of the cast-iron historic districts, where fire escapes animate the buildings' façades. The spirit of New York is to be found among canyons formed by skyscrapers, between masterpieces of civil engineering suspended over the Hudson and East River. It hangs in the air amid the trees of the vast and verdant Central Park, where 19th-century landscape designers worked miracles re-creating a space where even inner-city dwellers could enjoy hills, lakes, streams, bridle paths and footpaths for strolling and jogging. A few years ago the park was suffering from severe neglect but today - thanks to funds

126-127 and 127 top At the corner of Broadway and 42nd Street, Times Square is completely different from the typically European conception of a square. But its lights, moving advertising messages and, above all, the great New Year celebration, sponsored by The New York Times, make it popular with New Yorkers and tourists alike.

127 bottom Times Square gets ready for the long New York night. Here we have a concentration of cinemas, theatres, restaurants, shops and striptease clubs, all aiming to stupefy and attract an audience.

128 left The Chrysler Building provides one of the most fascinating nocturnal sights of the entire city.

128 right At night the lights make the Empire State Building visible even from a considerable distance, amid a series of brilliantly coloured layers of light.

put together by a group of benefactors, and the efforts of many volunteers - its fountains and Art Deco are attentively preserved, its lawns carefully tended. Solitary walks are admittedly not advisable at certain times of day and in certain places, but New Yorkers in their thousands have rediscovered the city's green heart and flock here in summer for big musical and theatrical events. It's as though they want to re-gain possession of a space they consider their very own.

129 Here we see the thousand lights of New York, the city-spectacle, ready to extend a welcome to all those who can adapt to its rules and rhythms, just like many famous figures and fortune seekers of the past have done before them.

130-131 Electric lighting has always done generous service to the city of New York. At night, the town seems to come alive with millions of artificial stars, which emphasise the outlines of the most famous monuments.

INDEX

Page numbers followed by "c" refer to captions.

A

Africa, 51c
Albany, 39, 39c, 44c, 55c
Algonquin Hotel, 24, 89
Algonquins, 24, 25, 29
Alice Tully Hall, 116c
Allen, Woody, 12, 103
Alma Mater, statue, 16c, 116c
Amendement, the 18th, 52, 52c
America, 27, 33, 39c, 41c, 44c, 50c, 51c, 63, 73, 97, 99c, 116, 119, 122, 125c
American Museum of Natural History, 110, 110c, 111c
American Revolution, 30, 73
American War of Independence, 34, 35, 60c
Amsterdam, 89
Amsterdam Avenue, 116
Andrew Fletcher, paddlewheeler, 73
Anne, Queen of England, 30
Antwerp, 89
Apollo Theater, 118c
Arab, picture, 107c
Architectural League, 57c
Arden, Elizabeth, 98c
Arnold Constable, 84
Art Deco, 12c, 73, 93, 94c, 97, 125, 128
Asia, 51c
Astor Court, 104
Astor, John Jacob, 83, 84c
Atlantic Ocean, 38c, 39, 41c, 121
Atlas, statue, 57c, 98c
Ausonia Hotel, 50c
Auster, Paul, 12
Avery Fisher Hall, 116c

B

Babe Ruth, 53
Ballangheri's, 125c
Barnard, George, 119, 119c
Barnes & Nobles, bookshop, 12c
Barrio, museum, 119
Barrymore, John, 110c
Bartholdi, Frédéric-Auguste, 60
Battery, the, 30, 30c, 33
Battery Park, 63
Bauhaus, 107c
Bayard Street, 76
Beatles, The, 116
Bedford Street, 83
Bedloe, Isaac, 60c
Bedloe's Island, 17c, 60c
Beijing, 76c

Bell, Alexander Graham, 41, 41c
Benchley, Robert, 89
Bergdorf Goodman, 98c
Bernstein, Leonard, 41c, 89, 116c
Bethesda Fountain, 44c
Bible, 44c, 116
Big Apple, 3c, 12, 59, 65, 122
Blaue Reiter, 107c
Bloomingdale, 98
Bombay, 47
Bonfire of the Vanities, 59, 59c, 97
Boston, 39, 60c
Boston Tea Party (16.12.1773), 34
Boston University, 41c
Bow Bridge, 112c
Breede Wegh, 28
Breetweg, 39c
Britain, 30
British Crown, 30, 30c, 34, 34c
British East India Company, 34
British Stamp Act, 34c
Broadway, 17, 28, 39c, 44c, 50c, 83, 84, 84c, 85c, 89, 126c, 127c
Bronck, Jonas, 28c
Bronx, 32c, 33, 45c, 47c, 48, 80c
Brooklyn, 41c, 43c, 45c, 48, 60, 73c, 121, 121c, 122
Brooklyn Bridge, 42c, 43c, 73, 73c, 76, 122c
Brooklyn Heights, 121, 121c
Brooklyn Museum, 121
Brooklyn, port of, 58c
Bryant Park, 39c
Building 636, 90c
Bulgari, jewellery, 98c
Burnham, Daniel H., 50c, 84
Butler Library, 116

C

California, 60
Calloway, Cab, 53, 119
Canal Street, 76c
Canova, Antonio, 16c
Canton, 76c
Capa, Robert, 110
Capone, Al, 53c
Capote, Truman, 98
Carnegie, Andrew, 40c, 41
Carnegie Hall, 40c, 41, 89, 89c
Castelli, Leo, 80
Castle Clinton, 63
Catlin, George, 24c
Cayuga, 25
Cedar Grove, 8
Central Park, 17, 42c, 44c, 47, 59, 101c, 104, 110, 110c, 112c, 113, 113c, 116, 127
Central Park Lake, 112c
Central Park North, 113c

Central Park South, 113c
Cézanne, Paul, 107c
Chagall, Marc, 109c
Champlain, Samuel de, 25, 25c
Charles II, King of England, 30, 30c
Charlevoix, 25
Chelsea, 84
Chelsea Hotel, 84
Cherry Hill, 112c
Chevrolet, 8
Chicago, 41
Children's Museum, 121
Children of Freedom, 34, 34c
China, 76
Chinatown, 76, 76c
Chinese New Year, 76
Chorus Line, musical, 89
Christian Dior, 98c
Chrysler Building, 55c, 86c, 94, 94c, 97c, 128c
Chrysler, Walter, 94
City Hall Park, 34c, 51c
Clermont, steamboat, 39, 39c
Cleveland, Grover, 44c
Cloisters, 119, 119c, 122
Coenties Slip, 45c
Colonnade Road, 83
Columbia School of Journalism, 116
Columbia University, 16c, 33, 33c
Columbia University Campus, 116
Columbus Circus, 89, 116c
Commissioner for Indian Affairs, 33
Committee of Public Health, 30, 30c
Common Council, 39
Coney Island, 17, 121
Confucius, plaza, 76
Conservatory Water, 113
Constitution, 52c, 63
Continental Congress, 34
Cooper-Hewitt Museum, 110
Cornbury, Lord, 30a, 33
Cosby, governor, 33, 33c
Costa Rica, 12
Cotton Club, 53, 119
Country Court House, 48c
Crystal Palace, 39, 39c
Cunard Building, 84c
Cuomo, Mario, 59, 59c, 78
Currier & Ives, 42c

D

Dairy, The, 113
Dakota Building, 47, 116
Dean & DeLuca, 80
Declaration of Independence, 34, 35c
Degas, Edgar, 107c
Delaunay, Robert, 109c

Delft, 32c
Democratic Convention, 55c
De Niro, Robert, 78
Depression, 53, 55c, 85c, 121
Dewey, George, 50c
De Witt, Clinton, 38c, 39,
Diamond Row, 89
Dinkins, Davis, 59, 59c
Dos Passos, John Roderigo, 83
Downtown Athletic Club, 73
Drinking Soldier, picture, 109c
Duke of York, 30
Dutch East India Company, 26c
Dutch West India Company, 27, 28c, 29
Dutch, 28c
Dutchman Breede Wegh, 28
Disney parks, 121

E

East River, 9c, 17c, 58c, 60c, 73, 73c, 94, 94c, 103, 127
East Village, 83
Egypt, 104c
Ellington, Duke, 118c
Ellis Island, 42c, 46, 46c, 60, 60c, 63
Empire State Building, 2c, 8c, 55, 56c, 57c, 65c, 84, 86c, 87, 94, 101c, 111c, 128c
England, 30, 30c
Erie Canal, 38c, 39
Erie, Lake, 38c
Europe, 30, 34, 39c, 41c, 47, 51c, 55, 60c, 122, 125c

F

Fascism, 55
Fashion Row, 41
Federal Hall National Monument, 63, 51c, 65c, 66c
Federal House, 51c
Federal Reserve Bank, 63
Fifth Avenue, 50c, 78, 84, 84c, 90, 90c, 93, 97, 97c, 98c, 99c, 109, 109c
Financial District, 63, 64, 122c
Flagg, Ernst, 50c
Flatiron Building, 50c, 84, 84c
Flegenheimer, Arthur, 53c
Fourth Avenue, 85c
France, 44c, 49, 60c, 119
Francis I, 27
Fraunces Tavern Museum, 73
French, 27, 33, 44c, 49
French Canada, 25c
French Crown, 27
French, Daniel Chester, 16c
Frick Collection, 110
Fuller Building, 50c

Fulton Fish Market, 73
Fulton, Robert, 39c, 39

G

Game of Cards, picture, 107c
Garment District, 84
Gauguin, Paul, 107c
General Electric Building, 90, 91c
George III, King of England, 34, 36c
Giuliani, Rudolph, 59, 59c
Gramercy Park, 84, 85c
Grand Army Plaza, 101c
Grand Central Terminal, 2c, 42c, 93, 93c
Grant, Cary, 83
Grant, President, 110c
Gray, Elisha, 41c
Great Lakes, 39
Great Oyster Island, 60c
Great Rotunda, 109
Great Spirit, 25
Great War, 52
Great White Way, 89
Greene Street, 80
Greenwich Village, 80, 83c
Grove Court, 83
Gucci, 98c
Guernica, 102c
Guggenheim, see Solomon Guggenheim
Gutenberg Bible, 90

H

Hair, musical, 83
Hale, Nathan, 35, 35c
Half Moon, 27
Hamilton, Alexander, 71c
Hard Rock Café, 125c
Hardenberg, H.J., 50c
Haring, K, 17c
Harlem, 13c, 59, 118c, 119, 122, 127
Harlem Heights, 37c
Harlem Urban Development Corporation, 122
Harley Davidson Café, 125c
Harmon, architect, 57c
Harvey, Charles T., 45c
Hayden Planetarium, 110
Helmsley Building, 94
Helmsley, Harry, 94
Helmsley, Leona, 94
Hepburn, Audrey, 98
Herald Square, 84
Hester Street, 47c
Hiawatha, 25, 25c
Hine, Lewis W., 48c
Holiday, Billy, 118c
Holland, 29, 29c

Hollywood, 89
Hood, Raymond, 90
Hopper, Edward, 83, 104
Houston Street, 80
Howe, William, general, 37c
Hudson River, 9c, 24, 29c, 39c, 58c, 60c, 63, 64, 64c, 73, 80, 116, 121c, 127
Hudson, Henry, 26c, 27, 121c
Hunt, Howland, 104c
Hunt, Richard Morris, 104c

I

Impressionism, 107c
Indians: - Algonquian, 24c
- Chippeway, 24c, 26c
- Iroquois, 24, 24c
- Onondaga, 25c
- Wickquesgeek, 28c
International Building, 57c
International Center of Photography (ICP), 110
Iroquois League of Six Nations, 25
Island of Tears, 46, 60
Isozake, Arata, 80
Italian Renaissance, 89c

J

James, Duke of York, 30c
Jefferson Market Courthouse, 83
Jewish Museum, 110
Johnson, William, 33, 33c

K

Kandisnsky, Vasilij, 107c, 109, 109c
Keaton, Diane, 103
King, Charles Bird, 24
King Kong, film, 56c, 87
King's College, 33, 33c
Klee, Paul, 103c, 107c
Koch, Ed, 58c, 59

L

Ladies' Mile, 84
Lady Liberty, see Statue of Liberty
Lafayette Street, 78
La Guardia, Fiorello, 55, 55c, 59, 90
Lamb, William, 8c, 57c
Lawrie Lee, 57c, 91c, 94c, 101c
Lazarus, Emma, 60
Léger, Fernand, 109c
Leisler, Jacob, 30, 30c
Lennon, John, 47, 116
Lenox Avenue, 118c, 119c
Lenox, James, 84c

133

Les Demoiselles d'Avignon, picture, 102c, 103
Levi's Store, 125c
Liberty Island, 17c
Liberty Tree, 34c
Lichtenstein, Roy, 109c
Lincoln Center, 116, 116c,
Little Flower, see La Guardia, Fiorello
Little Italy, 46, 60, 76c, 78
Lockport, 38c
Loire, river, 78
London, 8, 39
Longacre Square, 88c
Long Island, 37c
Lord & Taylor, 84
Los Angeles, 125c
Low Library of Columbia University, 16c, 116c
Lower East Side, 46, 47c, 76, 76c, 78
Lower Manhattan, 29, 60, 66c, 73
Lower Midtown, 94c
Lower Plaza, 90c
Lyceum Theater, 89

M

Macy's, 13c, 39, 44c, 84
Madison Square, 84, 104
Madison Square Garden, 88c, 89
Madrid, 102c
Malcom X Avenue, 118c
Manhattan, 2c, 26c, 28, 30, 43c, 48, 59, 65c, 73c, 80, 86c, 94c, 112c, 113c, 119, 119c
Manhattan Bridge, 73c
Manhattan, film, 12, 103
Manhattan Island, 8c, 9c, 28c, 41c, 58c, 60, 60c, 64
Maritime Craft Center, 73
Marilyn in Gold, painting, 103c
McEvans, James, 34c
MetLife Building, 93c, 94
Metropolitan Museum of Art, 16c, 104, 104c, 107c
Metropolitan Opera House, 89, 116, 116c
Meucci, Antonio, 41c
Midtown, 89
Midtown Building, 2c
Midwest, 39
Minissais, 60c
Minuit, Peter, 28, 64
Miró, Joan, 109c
Modigliani, Amedeo, 109c
Mohawk, 25
MOMA, see Museum of Modern Art
Monet, Claude, 103, 104c
Morgan, Pierpont, 40c

Mould, J. Wrey, 104c,
Mulberry Street, 47c, 78c
Museo del Barrio, 119
Museum Mile, 104
Museum of Immigration, 46
Museum of Modern Art, 102c, 103, 103c

N

Naples, 78c
National Academy of Design, 110
Nazism, 55
Netherlands, 29c
New Albany, 28
New Amsterdam, 26c, 28, 28c, 29, 29c, 30, 30c, 31c, 63
New Deal, 53c, 55
New Jersey, 8
New Netherlands, 29
New York 2, 8, 8c, 12, 12c, 17, 17c, 24, 24c, 26c, 27, 30, 30c, 33, 34, 35, 35c, 36c, 37c, 38c, 39c, 41, 41c, 43c, 44c, 46, 47, 47c, 48, 50c, 51c, 52c, 53, 55c, 57c, 58c, 59, 59c, 60, 60c, 63, 64, 71c, 73, 73c, 76, 76c, 78, 80, 80c, 83, 83c, 84, 84c, 86c, 87, 89, 89c, 90, 94, 94c, 101c, 103c, 104c, 109c, 110, 119, 122c, 125, 125c, 127, 128c
New York Bay, 60c
New York City Museum, 110, 110c, 111c
New Yorker, 89
New York Gazette, 33
New York Herald, newspaper, 84
New York Philarmonic Orchestra, 40c
New York Public Library, 39c, 84c, 90
New York Shakespeare Festival, 83
New York State, 34c, 39, 55, 55c, 59c
New York State Theater, 116c
New York Stock Exchange, 63, 64c
New York Times, 88c, 127c
New York University, 80, 83c
New York Weekly Journal, 33, 33c
New World, 30, 46, 119
Niagara Falls, 73
Nicholls, Richard, Colonel, 30, 30c, 31c
Normandy, 107c
North America, 25c
North Brooklyn, 122c
Northwest Passage, 27
NYSE, 63

O

Old Continent, 46, 119
Old Merchant's House, 83
Olmsted, Frederick Law, 113c

Oneida, 25
Onondaga, 25
Ono, Yoko, 116
Orchard Street, 76

P

Pan Am Building, 93c, 94
Paramount, 125
Paris, 125c
Paris Opera House, 93
Park Avenue, 12c, 94, 104
Parker, Dorothy, 89
Park Slope, 120c
Pennsylvania Hotel, 52c
Pennsylvania Station, 88c
Philadelphia, 34, 35c, 39
Picasso, Pablo, 17, 102c, 103, 109
Pierpont Morgan J., collection, 94
Pierpont Morgan Library, 84c, 94
Playing with Thirteen, picture, 103c
Plaza Hotel, 98, 125
Preparedness, picture, 109c
Prince Street, 80c
Prohibitionism, 52, 52c, 53c
Prometheus, statue, 17c, 90, 90c, 101c
Public Theater, 83
Pulitzer Prize, 116

Q

Queens, 45c, 48, 58c
Queensboro Bridge, 58c, 103

R

Radio City Music Hall, 89c, 90
Rainbow Room, 90
Ramble, The, 112c
RCA Building, 56c, 57c
Renaissance, 73
Renoir, Pierre-Auguste, 107c
Répétition d'un Ballet sur Scène, picture, 107c
Reservoir Park, 39c
Richmond, 48
Richmond, Battle of, 35
Riverside, 116
Roaring Twenties, 53
Rockefeller Center, 17c, 55, 57c, 89c, 90, 90c, 91c, 98c, 101c
Rockefeller, John D., Jr., 57c, 90, 94, 94c, 119
Roebling, John A., 43c
Roebling, Washington, 73
Rohe, Mies, van der, 17, 97
Rome, 8

Roosevelt, Franklin Delano, 53c, 55, 55c, 121
Roosevelt Island, 58c
Ross, Harold, 89
Rotterdam, 39
Russian Tea Room, 89, 127

S

Saks, 98c
San Gennaro, feast day, 46, 78, 78c
Sant'Antonio of Padua, feast day, 78, 78c
Schmerhorn Row, 73
Schomburg Center for Research into Black Culture, 119
Schubert Theater, 89
Scorsese, Martin, 78
Scotland, 40c
Sculpture Garden, 103
Seabury Commission, 52
Seagram Building, 17, 97
Seaport, 120c
Second World War, 59
Seneca, 25
Shangai, 12
Shakespeare in the Park, theatrical performance, 113
Sherman, General, 101c
Shreve, architect, 57c
Singer Building, 2c, 50c
Sixth Avenue, 41
Sleepless in Seattle, film, 56c
Smith, Al, 55c
SoHo, 80, 80c, 122
Solomon Guggenheim Museum, 17, 80, 109, 109c
Sons of Liberty, 34
South of Houston, see SoHo
South Street Seaport, 73c
South Street Seaport Museum, 73, 73c
Spain, 48c, 119
Spanish-American War, 50c
Spielberg, Steven, 98
St. John the Divine, 42c, 116, 116c
St. Luke's Place, 83, 83c
St. Mark's-in-the-Bowery Church, 83
St. Nicholas District, 118c
St. Patrick's Cathedral, 78, 96c, 97, 99c
Stamp Act, 34, 34c
Stamp Act Congress, 34
Stanford White, 80
Starck, Philippe, 125
Starry Night, picture, 103, 103c
Stars and Stripes, 37c
Statue of Liberty, 17c, 44c, 49, 60, 60c, 63, 128c, 136c
Statue of Peace, 94c
Stokowski, Leopold, 89
Stonemasons' House, 116
Strawberry Fields, 116
Studio Museum, 119
Stuyvesant, Family, 83
Stuyvesant, Peter, 29, 30, 30c
Stuyvesant Square, 84
Sutton Place, 58c
Sylvia's, 127

T

Tammany Hall, 48
Tarsus, 104c
Temple of Dendur, 104, 104c
Temporary Emergence Relief Administration, 55
Thanksgiving Day, 17, 84
Theater District, 89, 89c, 90, 122
Theater Row, 122c
Tiffany's, 12, 98, 98c
Tilden, Samuel Jones, 84c
Times Square, 88c, 89, 89c, 122c, 125, 127c
TKTS, 17
Toscanini, Arturo, 41c, 89
Treaty of Paris (1783), 33, 35
Tredwell, Seabury, 83
Triangle Below Canal, see TriBeCa
Triangle Shirtwaist Company, 48c, 49
TriBeCa, 80, 122
Trinity Church, 36c, 63, 65c
Trump, Donald, 97
Trump Tower, 97, 97c
Tuscaroras, 25
Tweed Courthouse, 48
Twin Towers of Central Park West, 116
Tweed William March "Boss", 48, 48c

U

Union Square, 84, 85c
Unites Nations Building, 17c
United Nations Headquarters, 94, 94c
Unites Nations Organisation, 94c
United States, 33, 39, 40c, 41, 48, 51c, 53c, 55, 59, 59c, 60c, 63, 65c, 78c, 83, 94, 94c, 97, 116c, 119, 121c
United States Custom House, 51c, 71c, 73
Upper East Side, 104
Upper West Side, 116
Upper Midtown, 97, 103
U.S.A., see United States

V

Van Cortland House, 32c, 33
Van Cortland, Frederick, 32c
Vanderbilt, Cornelius, 42c
Van Gogh, Vincent, 103, 103c, 104
Vaux, Calvert, 104c, 113c
Verona, 8
Verrazzano, Giovanni da, 26c, 27
Volstead Act, 52c
Vuchetich, Eugeny, 17c, 94

W

Waldorf Astoria Hotel, 12c, 97, 125
Walker, James J., 52, 53, 53c
Wall of Democracy, 76
Wall Street, 29, 39, 51c, 53, 59, 59c
Wall Street Crash, 53c, 63
Wargemont, 107c
War of Independence, 39, 39c
Warhol, Andy, 103c
Warsaw, 12
Washington, George, 35, 35c, 37c, 51c, 63, 65c, 83
Washington Heights, 119
Washington Square, 80, 83c
Water Lilies, picture, 103
Weekquaesgeek, 29c
West, 39c
West Broadway, 80
West Point, 39c
West Side Story, musical, 116c
Wharton, Edith, 41, 83, 84
Whitney Museum of American Art, 110
Wildlife Conservatory Center, 113
Williams, Colonel, 122c
Williamsburg, 122, 122c
Window on the World restaurant, 64
Winter Garden, 62, 64, 64c
Wolfe, Tom, 59, 59c, 97
Wollman Rink, 101c
Woolworth Building, 51c, 86c
Woolworth, Frank, 51c
World Financial Center, 62, 63c, 64, 64c
World Trade Center, 9c, 13c, 17c, 63c, 64c, 136c
World War I, 85c
World War II; 89
Wright, Frank Lloyd, 17, 109, 109c
Wyatt, Earp, 85c

Y

Young Man in a Blue Jacket, picture, 109c

Z

Zeppelin, airship, 55c, 17
Zenger, John Peter, 33, 33c

136 The Statue of Liberty seems to salute the twin towers, the twin giants of the World Trade Center.

Map from 1997 Edition © 1989 UNIQUE MEDIA™- Toronto Fax 416-924-7322

ILLUSTRATION CREDITS

Cover: Antonio Attini / Archivio White Star.

Back cover:
Antonio Attini / Archivio White Star: top left, center top left, center top right, center bottom left, center bottom right.
Cesare Gerolimetto: top left, bottom left, bottom right.

Antonio Attini / Archivio White Star: pages 3/6, 8 top, 8-9, 9 top, 12 top and bottom, 16, 17, 60 top and bottom, 61, 62-63, 65 top, 65 right, 67/70, 71, 72, 73, 77 top, 78 right, 84 left, 85 bottom left, 86-87, 88 top, 89 top right, 90, 91 top, 93 top, 94 left, 96-97, 97 top and bottom, 98 top left, 99, 104, 104-105, 105 top right, 108-109, 109 top left, 110, 111, 114-115, 117, 121 bottom, 126-127.
Marcello Bertinetti / Archivio White Star: pages 10-11, 76 top, 78 left, 79, 83 top right, 115 top, 120-121, 121 top.
AISA / Ag. Luisa Ricciarini: pages 30-31, 35 top left, 37 center right.
AKG Photo: pages 28-29 center and bottom, 39 bottom, 40-41, 41 center, 44 center, 44 bottom, 45 top left, 50 bottom right, 52 top right, 54 top right, 54-55, 102, 103 bottom left, 103 right, 106, 107, 108 top, 109 bottom left, 109 right.
Archivio White Star: pages 24, 26 bottom.
A.W.C. Images / Ag. SIE: pages 80 top, 80-81, 128 bottom.
Stefano Amantini / Atlantide: pages 14-15, 64 top, 76-77, 82, 83 bottom left, 89 top, 115 bottom, 118, 119, 122 top left, 122 top and center right.
Stefano Amantini / SIE: page 83 top left.
Sandra Baker / Liason International / Ag. Speranza: pages 63, 81 top left.
Udo Bernhard / Overseas: page 13 top.
Bruce Byers / Ag. Marka: pages 116-117.
Corbis-Bettmann Archive: pages 2 and 7 background, 25 top, 26 top left, 26-27, 27 top right, 32 top, 32-33, 33 top and bottom, 34 top, 34 bottom, 35 bottom, 37 top, 37 center left, 37 bottom, 38 top, 38-39, 39 top, 40 top right, 41 bottom, 45 top right, 45 center, 46 bottom right, 47 left, 47 bottom right, 48, 49 bottom, 50 top right, 50 center, 51 bottom, 52 bottom left, 52 bottom right, 55, 56, 56-57, 57, 59 bottom left, 59 right.
Stefano Cellai: pages 66, 94 right, 126 top, 127 bottom.
Giovanni Dagli Orti: pages 36 bottom, 36-37.
Lee Day / Black Star: page 90 center.
E.T. Archive: page 30 bottom.
F.P.G. International / Ag. Marka: pages 40 top left, 44 top, 46 top right, 46 center left, 46 bottom left, 47 center right, 50 top left, 51 top, 53 top left, 54 top left, 59 top left, 59 center left.
Fototeca Storica Nazionale: pages 42-43, 43 bottom, 51 bottom right, 52 top left.
Cesare Gerolimetto: pages 2 and 7 foreground, 12 center, 12-13, 64-65, 76 bottom, 80 center and bottom, 85 top right, 88-89, 92-93, 93 bottom, 97 center, 98 top left, 98 bottom right, 100-101, 112 top, 112-113, 113 center, 120 top, 122 bottom right, 124.
HP Huber / World Images / SIME: pages 90-91.
Andrea Iemolo: page 85 left.
Erica Lansner / Black Star: page 103 top left.
Mary Evans Picture Library: pages 25 center and bottom, 29 top and bottom, 30 top, 31 top, 34 center, 42 bottom left, 42 bottom right, 53 bottom left.
M. Mastrolillo / Ag. SIE: pages 74-75, 98 bottom left.
Museum of the City of New York: pages 27 top left, 28 top, 29 center, 39 center, 41 top, 46 top left, 47 top right, 58 top.
Lisa Quinones / Black Star: page 89 center.
Per Anders Pettersson / Black Star: page 127 top.
Andrea Pistolesi: pages 1, 18-19, 89 bottom right, 95, 128 top.
Photobank: pages 130-131.
Ag. Luisa Ricciarini: pages 35 top right, 42 top, 43 right, 48-49, 53 top left.
Michael Schwerberger / Das Photoarchiv: pages 62 top, 83 bottom right, 96 top, 105 top right.
P. Sclarandis / SIE: page 81 top right.
Giovanni Simeone / World Images / SIE: pages 20-21, 129.
Emilio F. Simion / Ag. Luisa Ricciarini: page 26 top right.
Marc E. Smith: page 122 bottom left.
Gianluigi Sosio: pages 116, 123, 125.
The Kobal Collection: page 58 bottom.
The Pierpont Morgan Collection: page 84 left.
Tom Sobolik / Black Star: page 136.